Leaving
LO DEBAR

RHONDA K. HOLLAND

CONTENTS

INTRODUCTION

A COVENANT is a binding, solemn agreement and commitment. It is not to be entered lightly, and it is to be cherished and highly regarded by the recipient.

This study will remind us of the results and blessings of such a covenant that was made between David and Jonathan. But it also is about the adventurous and not-so-pleasant journey getting there!

I have always loved the story of Mephibosheth recorded in **2 Samuel 9.** *Please read this passage before beginning this study.* We will discuss the individuals who are significant to the events that unfold. Of course, King David and Mephibosheth are the focus of the passage. Yet there is one unnamed person briefly mentioned before the ninth chapter who played a significant role and caught my attention—the nurse who dropped Mephibosheth. We read a brief statement about her earlier in **2 Samuel 4:4**.

> Jonathan, Saul's son, had a son who was a cripple in his feet. He was five years old when the news came out of Jezreel [of the deaths] of Saul and Jonathan. And the boy's nurse took him up and fled; and in her haste, he fell and became lame. His name was Mephibosheth (2 Samuel 4:4 AMPC).

We will consider this unnamed nurse and how she was identified by her failure. After all, in her haste she dropped what she was responsible for. And as a result there was heart-rending brokenness!

Then, there was the broken one, Mephibosheth, who was wounded at no fault of his own and suffered because of someone else's mistake. As a result, he ended up residing in a place called Lo Debar.

Lo Debar means "no pastures—a place of desolation." Who wants to live in a barren desolate place of no harvest or productivity? The word desolate means "to be devoid of inhabitants and visitors, bereaved, forsaken or abandoned, joyless, and sorrowful—a place of separation and darkness."

It was in such a place that Mephibosheth found himself, both literally and spiritually. Likely, his nurse was living there with him. What a sad pair they must have been!

But one day; one intentional God-ordained day, everything changed for Mephibosheth. David, the covenant-keeping king came into his world!

Perhaps you have found yourself in your own personal, spiritual or emotional Lo Debar. You have experienced days or seasons of joyless desolation. Maybe you cannot seem to forgive yourself for your own failures, and now you walk under condemnation. Or you may be hurt and even angry because someone caused brokenness in your spirit. Possibly, you are there and do not understand how you arrived or what led you to this place. Regardless of why or how you arrived, remember, your Lo Debar is temporary and there is a way out!

As you go through the pages of this study and look to the Word, it is my heart's desire that you will rejoice knowing no matter where you are at the moment, you have Jesus, your Covenant-Keeping King who is mindful of you.

And one day, one intentional God-ordained day everything will change for you and you will find yourself leaving Lo Debar.

Week 1
POWER TRUTH

"IT'S ALL MY FAULT"

The Condemnation Connection to Lo Debar
2 Samuel 4:4

As you study this week's lesson, sincerely search your heart and ask God to set you free from areas where you may give in to condemnation. Always be mindful that condemnation is a direct connection to your own Lo Debar.

Memorize **Romans 8:1**. Do not allow a Condemnation Connection in your life.

There is therefore now no condemnation to those who are in Christ Jesus, who do not walk according to the flesh, but according to the Spirit (Romans 8:1 NKJV).

"IT'S ALL MY FAULT"

The Condemnation Connection to Lo Debar
2 Samuel 4:4

> Jonathan, Saul's son, had a son who was a cripple in his feet. He was five years old when the news came out of Jezreel [of the deaths] of Saul and Jonathan. And the boy's nurse took him up and fled; and in her haste, he fell and became lame. His name was Mephibosheth (2 Samuel 4:4 AMPC).

CONDEMNATION is the expression of very strong disapproval. And sometimes the one who condemns you the most is you. Condemnation breeds disdain. And having self-disdain is a terrible way to live.

The word *disdain* means "to look on with scorn, to treat with contempt as being of little worth or consequence."

How many times do we belittle and beat up ourselves over mistakes, failures and sins committed until we convince ourselves that we deserve to be sad or hurt or even mistreated? We make no room for our own forgiveness and restoration. We begin to dwell on negative thoughts about ourselves. Then we openly and privately criticize our faults until we successfully create a habitually condemning mindset causing us to spiral into a pit of self-worthlessness and defeat.

Yes, when you think condemning thoughts about yourself enough, you will begin to hear yourself "say it." You will truly believe your own self-evaluations. And what began as "just a thought" develops into words and actions. If that thought life is not defeated, it creates a joyless place of sorrow, desolation and darkness.

Sorrow and desolation may give way to an atmosphere void of good expectations. When there is no expectation, all anticipation of something better is gone. Real productivity is virtually impossible. If hope is present, it may be just barely alive. Survival is your only goal. Condemnation has become your connection, your inroad, to your own personal Lo Debar. Once you find yourself there, it feels like there is no way out.

Remember the meaning of Lo Debar, "no pastures—a place of desolation." No pastures means no harvest. The word desolate means "to be devoid of inhabitants and visitors, bereaved, forsaken or abandoned, joyless, and sorrowful—a place of separation."

Condemnation is cruel. It does not care that it leaves its victim desolate and in despair.

In **2 Samuel 4:4**, we discover the reason why Mephibosheth was "broken." This one verse helps us understand the desperation of the moment. Word had come home that both Saul, Mephibosheth's grandfather, and Jonathan, his father, were killed in the same battle. The nurse who cared for little Mephibosheth—who was only five years old at the time—was immediately and understandably fearful. Her fear was generated because it was the custom that when battles were lost, the victorious opposing army would also come to the reigning king's home and kill those next in line to the throne. In this case, that would have been young Mephibosheth.

Mephibosheth's nurse, no doubt, loved him. Probably, she had been his nurturing caregiver all of his life. Perhaps she watched him grow from an infant to a happy and healthy little boy. She was the one he would turn to for comfort, affection and, now, protection.

In one unfolding situation, everything turned chaotic. Dreaded apprehension and fear filled the atmosphere. It was in a moment of horrific panic and haste, imagining the worst scenario, when the nurse took him and fled. Likely she was attempting to go to a place of refuge. Somehow, during their attempt to escape, Mephibosheth was injured and became lame. Some commentaries on this passage say he was likely dropped. Now, a horrible situation has just become worse.

Imagine with me what it must have felt like for this nurse. Filled with fear in an emotional moment, she reacted to the situation and fled in haste.

Have you found yourself reacting in haste when faced with an emotional crisis? Can you look back on a time when you made a decision you regretted that could have had a different outcome, had you waited and responded after thinking it through? Do you have a critical mindset towards yourself for reacting largely on your emotions? Are you now dealing with condemnation because of it? Have you actually stepped deeper into self-disdain?

These are hard things we must ask ourselves. We cannot allow condemnation and self-disdain to thrive in our heart. If we do, we will continue to live in our own personal Lo Debar, and we will never reap the amazing benefits of fully walking in the covenant blessings that Christ's love provides for us.

POINTS TO PONDER

I often say and will share it again in this study, that we have a cunning enemy who uses current events to give us careless emotions. The subtlety of our enemy is frequently used to create circumstances to come our way for the purpose of bringing a crisis into our lives. It is his intent to cause us, in our emotions, to react to the situation at hand and not respond in wisdom.

Emotions are the shallowest part of who we are. Emotions are fleeting and often leave as quickly as they come. In one moment we can become frightened and alarmed. We may temporarily lose real perspective; and it is then that our ability to make wise choices can be delayed until our emotions settle. There are times if we truly collect our thoughts and evaluate the situation before us, fear can almost dissipate as quickly as it comes. Always, we must guard against displaying emotionally charged reactions in the midst of a crisis. Our emotions can cause recklessness.

So decisions can be careless when based only on how we feel in the heat of the battle. To stop the enemy from gaining ground when we are in a battle, we must condition ourselves to respond but not react. Most battles attack and affect us emotionally. So we must be constantly aware of his tactic that causes us to react instead of respond! Otherwise, we may find ourselves on our way to a residency in Lo Debar.

Let's go back to the nurse. Now, she blames herself for Mephibosheth's physical pain and brokenness. She was not a bad or careless person. Considering the traditional image of nurses, she was just the opposite. After all, she was chosen to care for the reigning king's grandson, future heir to the throne. She would have had an excellent resumé. All the right credentials would have followed her name. And now, it all came to this—utter failure! She had dropped what she was responsible for (a little child) and literal brokenness became the result.

Consequently, her entire outlook changed.

⚹ She had been nurturing the one whom she believed would one day be king. And now, her hopes for him had been cruelly crushed. Because Mephibosheth was lame, as unfair as it was, he would now be considered unfit for court much less for becoming king. He would never live in a palace. He would live in exile. And so would she.

Yes, all in one dreaded moment, all because of circumstances she didn't control, everything had changed forever. Her emotions had overridden her better judgment and in her haste, she made a mistake. A mistake that hurt her also caused one she loved dearly to suffer. This created the perfect atmosphere for condemnation that could ultimately turn to self-disdain.

Perhaps you can identify with her. Maybe you feel you've dropped something you were responsible for and others have suffered because of it. You find yourself walking in a constant state of disappointment. Yes, you hide it well for the most part and only those closest to you are aware. As time passes, perhaps you still have not dealt with the underlying issues of your own condemnation. It is becoming increasingly harder and harder to cover your own lack of self-worth. You feel like a failure and it does not seem like it will ever change. You never meant for it to happen, and you feel you are the reason it did. You are beginning to feel like you will never leave Lo Debar. The wounds that hurt you the most are self-inflicted, and you feel you deserve the pain. Worse, since you blame yourself for being in Lo Debar, you feel as if you do not deserve a way out.

Truthfully, all we know for sure about this nurse is the scripture simply tells us "the boy's nurse took him up and fled; and in her haste, he fell and became lame." And so,

13

we immediately identify her with failure. When the story of Mephibosheth is taught, she is most often barely mentioned in the sermon or lesson. When she is, the speaker tends to point back to her as the one responsible for the brokenness of Mephibosheth. *Her failure becomes her identity.* She was in a hurry because she was afraid and she dropped him, so Mephibosheth was broken and wounded because of her.

Yes, this is all we know for sure about her. All else is speculation and imagination. But, oh! How speculation and imagination also come into play with us when we identify ourselves with our failures!

When speculation and imagination take over in negative ways, we begin to allow the worst scenarios to unfold in our minds. God gave us our imaginations to use in good ways. He has given us the ability to be creative and to accomplish so many things. And creativity first begins with an imaginary thought.

However, when we allow the enemy to use our imagination, he always intends to bring fear to the forefront; and a fearful imagination gives way to destruction and devastation.

God wants us to use our imagination to create dreams and goals. The devil intends to use that same imagination to destroy in us what God intends to create.

God wants your imagination to birth creativity. The devil wants your imagination to birth condemnation. What a contrast!

Let's read a familiar passage of Scripture that references our imagination.

> For though we walk in the flesh, we do not war after the flesh: (For the weapons of our warfare are not carnal, but mighty through God to the pulling down of strongholds;) Casting down imaginations, and every high thing that exalteth itself

against the knowledge of God, and bringing into captivity every thought to the obedience of Christ (2 Corinthians 10: 3-5 KJV).

It is both interesting and important to note that the first thing Paul says to do with the weapons we have been given for spiritual warfare is to <u>cast down imaginations</u>. Negative imaginations that contradict the Word of God and those that exalt themselves against the knowledge of God create strongholds in our minds. One such stronghold is the prison of condemnation and self-disdain.

It is a process not happening overnight. One thought, one imagined scenario at a time, begins the construction of our stronghold. When we identify ourselves with our failures, we begin to imagine ourselves as defeated and useless. <u>Fear of repeating failure overrides our desire to step out of our comfort zone.</u> Then we do not see ourselves as valuable. When we feel useless, we then begin to feel worthless and unloved. Loneliness and depression creep in. Condemnation over our failures takes center stage in our mind.

You may find yourself making statements about yourself, such as:

- "It's all my fault."
- "I deserve this! I brought it on myself."
- "I am not smart enough."
- "I can't do what other people do."
- "I'm just a failure."
- "God could never use someone like me."

If so, take a moment and write a prayer from your heart asking God to help you to stop speaking condemnation over yourself:

_____

_____

_____

_____

_____

_____

_____

When we constantly identify with our failures it affects the following:

- **Walk**
- **Worth**
- **Words**
- **Witness**
- **Worship**

Let's look at this list closely.

MY WALK

My **walk** with God is important for so many reasons. Simply stated, when you walk with someone you are obviously going in the same direction. You also communicate with the one you walk with daily. You learn their ways and develop a relationship.

God has a plan for your life unfolding often, one step at a time, but when you are in a constant state of feeling like a failure, you make little-to-no progress. You feel as if you are standing still, going nowhere. Truthfully, condemnation makes you fearful to move ahead, because you anticipate another failure on the horizon.

But remind yourself of this truth: God has chosen a plan and a path for you. This path leads to a destination and purpose He has created just for you. But His perfect plan for your life cannot be obtained if you are living in Lo Debar--all because you feel condemned.

> The steps of a good man are ordered by the Lord, And He delights in his way. Though he fall, he shall not be utterly cast down; For the Lord upholds him with His hand (Psalm 37:23-24 NKJV).

Look carefully at **Psalm 37:23-24**. *What about this passage gives you hope and encouragement?*

_____

_____

_____

_____

_____

_____

_____

Stop allowing past failures or current situations seeming like defeat to hold you back. These verses in Psalm 37 remind us of two important truths. (1) Your steps are directed by God and when you fall, He will lift you back up because He is holding your hand. (2) Do not focus on your failures, focus on the promise that He will walk with you every step of this journey called life. Observe by faith who is holding your hand.

Another passage that has become so dear to my heart is found in the book of Micah.

> But as for me, I will look to the Lord and confident in Him I will keep watch; I will wait with hope and expectancy for the God of my salvation; my God will hear me. Rejoice not against me, O my enemy! When I fall, I shall arise; when I sit in darkness, the Lord shall be a light to me (Micah 7:7-8 AMPC).

These verses tell us that there are times we sit in darkness and occasions when we fall. But we must look to the Lord. Our confidence is in Him and Him alone. Your hope will be restored when you look to God and see Him as your Deliverer.

You might have stumbled in your walk, missed the mark and fallen short of your goals. Perhaps you have strayed and even committed willful sin, but you do not have to accept defeat or failure. Yet, you must not stay down. Acknowledge your mistakes and repent of willful sin. See yourself as getting up and walking on with God.

When you fall, you will arise. Don't see yourself as down and out. See yourself as either up or getting up. Darkness will flee from your path, and His light will shine before you! Allow His presence to put a spring back in your step.

Stop allowing condemnation to affect your walk with God.

MY WORTH

1-24-19

✳ Let's talk about how condemnation causes a lack of self-worth. The enemy slips in and makes you feel God's acceptance of you is because of what you do for Him. Then he may constantly remind you of your failures. This makes you feel inadequate and fearful. To add to that list, you get the feeling of being unlovable and worthless to God.

18

But think about this. **The price paid for something is what determines its real worth.** And you were purchased by the precious Blood of Jesus. The Father sent His Son to die for you. Your worth is immeasurable to God. It is not based on works. You cannot attribute your value because of what you have accomplished. Nor can you diminish your worth to Him based on your failures. He came that all could be saved. He saw you as His beloved child and He desired to redeem you. You are of great worth to Him.

Condemnation and constantly referencing your failures will cause you to feel worthless. But you were bought with a high price. These verses are a reminder of the cost of our redemption.

> ...knowing that you were not redeemed with corruptible things, like silver or gold, from your aimless conduct received by tradition from your fathers, but with the precious blood of Christ, as of a lamb without blemish and without spot (1 Peter 1:18-19 NKJV).

> And [now] they sing a new song, saying, You are worthy to take the scroll and to break the seals that are on it, for You were slain (sacrificed), and with Your blood You purchased men unto God from every tribe and language and people and nation (Revelation 5:9 AMPC).

Stop allowing condemnation to cause you to question your worth. You were purchased by His precious blood, making you *priceless to God.*

Remind yourself: The price paid for me is what determines my worth.

MY WORDS

Now, let's think about how condemnation affects our **words.** Years ago, I heard a minister make a statement I have never forgotten, and I say it quite often. *"If it's in the well, it's coming up in the bucket!"* How true it is! And everyone around in

19

earshot of your words has a taste of what you share from that bucket.

How you perceive yourself is developed first in your thoughts and imagination, as we have discussed. Then out of the abundance of your heart, your words come forth! Jesus tells us that people speak what is in their heart. Your mindset is revealed by what you say. Condemnation and self-disdain **will** surface in your conversations.

> A good man out of the good treasure of his heart brings forth good; and an evil man out of the evil treasure of his heart brings forth evil. For out of the abundance of the heart his mouth speaks (Luke 6:45 NKJV).

Think of this verse in Ephesians as instructions on how to speak about and to others. *But also apply it to how you converse about yourself.*

> Let no foul or polluting language, nor evil word nor unwholesome or worthless talk [ever] come out of your mouth, but only such [speech] as is good and beneficial to the spiritual progress of others, as is fitting to the need and the occasion, that it may be a blessing and give grace (God's favor) to those who hear it (Ephesians 4:29 AMPC).

In your own words, write down what you feel in your heart this passage speaks to you:

_____

_____

_____

_____

_____

My Mama used to say, **"Be Sweet"** every time I left the house and even after I became an adult. This is what she meant with those two little words of wisdom:

> Let all bitterness and indignation and wrath (passion, rage, bad temper) and resentment (anger, animosity) and quarreling (brawling, clamor, contention) and slander (evil-speaking, abusive or blasphemous language) be banished from you, with all malice (spite, ill will, or baseness of any kind). And become useful and helpful and kind to one another, tenderhearted (compassionate, understanding, loving-hearted), forgiving one another [readily and freely], as God in Christ forgave you (Ephesians 4:31 AMPC).

"Be Sweet." The world needs it now more than ever and you do make a difference. Make someone glad you crossed his/her path today.

Yes, I must guard how I speak about myself and others. Be honest and ask yourself this question. Do I criticize others by speaking statements like, "You know, he's the one that...." or "Remember, she is the one who..." If I am guilty of identifying someone by their faults, failures or sins, it is a form of condemnation that contradicts the instructions given in Ephesians 4: 31, 32.

Your ears hear your mouth speak Stop speaking death, discouragement and condemnation over yourself or others. Speak life and healing.

Death and life are in the power of the tongue, And those who love it will eat its fruit (Proverbs 18:21, NKJV).

Simply said, you speak either death or life, and since you do eat your words, you want to make sure they are sweet.

MY WITNESS

If my words are always negative and hurtful, then I no longer become an effective *witness* for Christ. My witness about Him to others must include my own testimony of His love, acceptance and forgiveness; or others by observing my example may not desire a relationship with Him. If my words are always condemning and negative toward myself, how can I convince others of His love for them? Thus, my witness for Him and of Him may become ineffective. And if my demeanor is always downcast and hopeless, why would someone want to follow my God? They already know and experience the feeling of hopelessness.

> Let the word of Christ dwell in you richly in all wisdom, teaching and admonishing one another in psalms and hymns and spiritual songs, singing with grace in your hearts to the Lord. And whatever you do in word or deed, *do* all in the name of the Lord Jesus, giving thanks to God the Father through Him (Colossians 3:16-17 NKJV).

Let your speech always *be* with grace, seasoned with salt, that you may know how you ought to answer each one (Colossians 4:6, NKJV).

My witness of Christ's redeeming love and grace must be a source of encouragement to others and to myself. I must share His plan of redemption in confidence that He has also done the same for me.

MY WORSHIP

A mindset of condemnation also affects my **worship**. If I cannot see Jesus as my personal Deliverer and Redeemer, I cannot truly worship Him for Who He really is. I cannot live my life as a true worshipper if I forget all that He has done for me.

Psalm 103 is our reminder not to forget.

> Bless the Lord, O my soul; And all that is within me, *bless* His holy name! Bless the Lord, O my soul, And forget not all His benefits: Who forgives all your iniquities, Who heals all your diseases, Who redeems your life from destruction, Who

crowns you with lovingkindness and tender mercies, Who satisfies your mouth with good *things, So that* your youth is renewed like the eagle's (Psalm 103:1-5 NKJV).

Take a moment and purposefully list some of the blessings God has freely given to you.

_____

_____

_____

_____

_____

_____

_____

Now, pause for a moment and thank Him for those benefits.

The Lord does not want you to walk under the burden of condemnation. Remind yourself of His goodness and mercy. Forget not all His benefits.

Another beautiful reminder of His loving care to us is found in a beloved and favorite passage from Romans 8.

There is therefore now no condemnation to those who are in Christ Jesus, who do not walk according to the flesh, but according to the Spirit (Romans 8: 1 NKJV).

He who did not spare His own Son, but delivered Him up for us all, how shall He not with Him also freely give us all things? Who shall bring a charge against God's elect? *It is* God who justifies. Who is he who condemns? It is Christ who died, and furthermore is also risen, who is even at the right hand of God, who also makes intercession for us. Who shall separate us from the love of Christ? *Shall* tribulation, or distress, or persecution, or famine, or nakedness, or peril, or sword? As it is written:

23

"For Your sake we are killed all day long;
We are accounted as sheep for the slaughter."

Yet in all these things we are more than conquerors through Him who loved us. For I am persuaded that neither death nor life, nor angels nor principalities nor powers, nor things present nor things to come, nor height nor depth, nor any other created thing, shall be able to separate us from the love of God which is in Christ Jesus our Lord (Romans 8:32-39 NKJV).

The eighth chapter of Romans is so beloved by Christians everywhere. Notice this beautiful and comforting passage begins with *"no condemnation"* and ends with *"no separation."* We are assured that there is "now" no condemnation to those who are in Christ; and we are reminded that nothing can separate us from His eternal love.

Condemnation is from the enemy Satan wants you to hold on to all the painful memories associated with your failures, mistakes and sins. He wants you to feel undeserving of pardon and forgiveness. But he is a liar and a thief. He wants to steal your joy and kill and destroy your future and purpose. He does not want you to receive the truth, because the truth is your way out of Lo Debar.

The same verse exposing the enemy's agenda tells you the truth about our Savior. Jesus desires for you to have an abundant and joyful life, both in this world and in the world to come.

The thief comes only in order to steal and kill and destroy. I came that they may have and enjoy life, and have it in abundance (to the full, till it overflows) (John 10:10 AMPC).

Read this verse in Romans and purpose in your heart that you will not allow condemnation to mold your mindset. Ask God to help you daily renew your thoughts according to His plan and love for you.

And do not be conformed to this world, but be transformed by the renewing of your mind, that you may prove what is that good and acceptable and perfect will of God (Romans 12:2 NKJV).

If you have struggled with condemnation, please **Pray** this **Prayer:**

"God, I come before You in the precious name of Your Son, Jesus, my Savior. Thank You that You have made a way out of condemnation for me. Thank You that Your forgiveness is extended to me and restoration is available to me. I do not have to live in a place of desolation created because of condemnation and self-disdain. I am forgiven and my sins are covered by the sacrificial blood of Jesus. I belong to you and You will heal my mind as I daily meditate on Your Word and the truth it presents. My condemnation connection to Lo Debar is broken. I will not stay in a place of spiritual desolation. I am free from the pain of condemnation. My mind is renewed through You."

In Jesus' name. Amen.

Take a few moments and praise God because there is NOW no condemnation and nothing can separate you from His love. You are forgiven and greatly loved. And you are set free by the power of Jesus Christ.

Therefore if the Son makes you free, you shall be free indeed (John 8:36, NKJV).

Remember, when we are faced with trials and failures in this life, condemnation will try to creep up on all of us. The enemy is constantly looking for a way to bring self-disdain in your mind through the weapon of condemnation, because it gives him access to your thought life. Guard against it. Do not let the enemy cause you to create a "condemnation connection to Lo Debar."

Spend time journaling this week and praise God daily for a renewed mind. Read and meditate on Romans 8. Speak life and truth! Rejoice because condemnation has no place in your life.

Be in prayer and preparation for next week's lesson as we look at the negative ways un-forgiveness affects us and how blame becomes **a Gateway to Lo Debar.**

Week 2

POWER TRUTH

"It's All Your Fault"

The Blame Game Gateway to Lo Debar

As you meditate on and study this week's lesson, remember that blame is an unfriendly and unkind word. Blame left unchecked brings un-forgiveness and bitterness.

Ask God to help you apply the instructions given in **Colossians 3:13**. Memorize and journal about this verse.

> Be gentle and forbearing with one another and, if one has a difference (a grievance or complaint) against another, readily pardoning each other; even as the Lord has [freely] forgiven you, so must you also [forgive] (Colossians 3:13 AMPC).

Week 2

"It's All Your Fault"

The Blame Game Gateway to Lo Debar
2 Samuel 4:4

BLAME is an unfriendly and unkind word. It is a word that attributes fault, responsibility and disapproval on someone often with the intent of making a person answerable for their actions. And when we are the victim of their wrongdoing, we tend to find it easy to pass judgment on the one we blame for causing us pain. Attributing blame, mixed with a judgmental spirit toward someone, can cause a mindset of un-forgiveness to flourish. And an unforgiving attitude gives birth to bitterness. Bitterness will cause you to live in Lo Debar; and if left unresolved, you will spend most of your time in the confines of that dreaded place of desolation.

Let's look again at the verse we discussed last week. In the first week of this study, our focus was the nurse identified with failure. Remember, maintaining a mindset of failure breeds condemnation and self-disdain.

This week, we will look at Mephibosheth and how the situation, played out in his life, could have caused the blame game to come into play. Blame often leads to a judgmental attitude and causes un-forgiveness to take root, producing the unpleasant fruit of bitterness.

> Jonathan, Saul's son, had a son who was a cripple in his feet. He was five years old when the news came out of Jezreel [of the deaths] of Saul and Jonathan. And the boy's nurse took him up and fled; and in her haste, he fell and became lame. His name was Mephibosheth (2 Samuel 4:4 AMPC).

Have you ever felt the brunt of someone's bad choice? Have you suffered at the hands of one who was supposed to care for you and love you? Possibly you were hurt by a parent, a spouse, or a trusted friend, mentor, or family member. Maybe you have suffered long because someone you truly care about let you down. So you feel "dropped and broken" because of it.

Just as condemnation and self-disdain can lead you to your own personal Lo Debar, so can un-forgiveness and bitterness when left unchecked in your heart.

There are times in our lives when we are genuinely hurt by someone's actions whether deliberate or unintentional. The pain can be overwhelming and disheartening to say the least. But please remember to forgive someone does not mean you are finding what they did to be acceptable. Forgiving someone is not tantamount to condoning what they did. Forgiveness is not an emotion. You may not even feel forgiveness at the moment you make the choice to do it. ***To forgive someone is a willful decision you make to obey God's instruction.*** Letting go of the role of judge toward the one you blame for your pain is liberating, and you will benefit greatly from it spiritually and emotionally. But holding on to it will cause you much sorrow.

In the Bible there are many references to give guidance in forgiving others. Let's take time and review just a few of them.

> Be gentle and forbearing with one another and, if one has a difference (a grievance or complaint) against another, readily pardoning each other; even as the Lord has [freely] forgiven you, so must you also [forgive] (Colossians 3:13 AMPC).

> And become useful and helpful and kind to one another, tenderhearted (compassionate, understanding, loving-hearted), forgiving one another [readily and freely], as God in Christ forgave you (Ephesians 4:32 AMPC).

> When angry, do not sin; do not ever let your wrath (your exasperation, your fury or indignation) last until the sun goes down. 27 Leave no [such] room or foothold for the devil [give no opportunity to him] (Ephesians 4:26 AMPC).

As you read these verses, write down what you feel may be some of the most important instructions concerning forgiveness:

_____

_____

_____

_____

_____

_____

_____

Each of these verses instructs us to make forgiving someone a "quick" work! The *Amplified Version* uses the word "readily" in Colossians 3:13 and again in Ephesians 4:32.

The Apostle Paul instructs us in Ephesians 4:26 not to let our anger cause us to sin. It is important to note that *anger is not a sin when there is a just cause,* but how we handle that anger is vital. We must control our anger, or our anger will control us. We are to deal with our anger before nightfall. Notice that when you follow Ephesians 4:27, you leave no room for the devil to gain a foothold on your mind. We must deal with our anger quickly so it will not provide the enemy such an opportunity.

If time passes, anger can become planted in your heart and quickly turn to blame which can lead to un-forgiveness. Then un-forgiveness can sprout into the root of bitterness. Bitterness is like a strong vine, spreading quickly, covering much ground and often choking the life out of everything it touches.

> Look after each other so that not one of you will fail to find God's best blessings. Watch out that no bitterness takes root among you, for as it springs up it causes deep trouble, hurting many in their spiritual lives (Hebrews 12:15 TLB).

Why do you think bitterness is so dangerous?

_____

_____

_____

_____

_____

All of us make choices that can affect others, either positively or negatively. This verse warns and reminds us when bitterness takes root, it springs up and causes deep trouble. It damages and hurts spiritually those who are touched by it.

Remember, Lo Debar means "no pastures—a place of desolation." The word *desolate* means "to be devoid of inhabitants and visitors, bereaved, forsaken or abandoned, joyless, and sorrowful—a place of separation and darkness."

A "spiritual" Lo Debar is a place of no lasting productivity. You cannot produce the fruit of the Spirit or reap a good harvest where the land is desolate with no pastures. So, nothing *good* grows in Lo Debar, *but the root of bitterness thrives there.*

To be unforgiving also stands in the way of an effective prayer life. Look at the solemn instruction Jesus gives in the book of Mark.

> And whenever you stand praying, if you have anything against anyone, forgive him and let it drop (leave it, let it go), in order that your Father Who is in heaven may also forgive you your [own] failings and shortcomings and let them drop. But if you do not forgive, neither will your Father in heaven forgive your failings and shortcomings (Mark 11:25-26 AMPC).

✶ Let's think about Mephibosheth again for a moment. He was born an heir to the throne! He was royalty and could have become king. But everything changed that fateful day he was dropped and became broken. His pain was not a "one-time occurrence." It was an on-going daily battle, causing him pain-- physically, spiritually and emotionally.

God's grace is required in order to extend forgiveness, especially when the pain continues. The help of our Heavenly Father is always available. A sufficient and generous dose of His amazing grace is provided to help you through your pain.

> But He said to me, My grace (My favor and loving-kindness and mercy) is enough for you [sufficient against any danger and enables you to bear the trouble manfully]; for My strength and power are made perfect (fulfilled and completed) and show themselves most effective in [your] weakness. Therefore, I will all the more gladly glory in my weaknesses and infirmities, that the strength and power of Christ (the Messiah) may rest (yes, may pitch a tent over and dwell) upon me! (2 Corinthians 12:9 AMPC).

This passage is such a comfort, and it is a beautiful reminder of God's love and grace abounding to us. Read and meditate on the power of this verse and know that God is with you and will enable you to forgive those who have hurt you.

He will lead you out one step at a time; with one dose of sufficient, always available, always adequate and always amazing grace.

You must choose to forgive in order to leave your spiritual Lo Debar. Let go of the blame game the enemy wants you to play. Remember, *blame and a judgmental spirit give way to un-forgiveness,* a poison to the one who harbors it. Once rooted, it spreads over into all other relationships, makes you question the motives of people and doubt their sincerity when they seek your friendship.

Because entertaining un-forgiveness can kindle skepticism towards others, it may cause you to build walls to keep people out--or at least at a safe distance away. Potentially, this may prevent real and beneficial friendships from developing.

Ironically, while un-forgiveness causes you to build walls that keep potential friendships out, it continually ties you to the one to whom you harbor blame and un-forgiveness. It is your constant awareness of them and the pain they caused which keep you within the confines of your personal Lo Debar.

That constant awareness in turn keeps the memories alive and the toxic thoughts rehearsed. And remember, what is in your heart comes out in your words. The more you think about it, the more likely you are to talk about it. The more you talk about it, the more alive the bitterly bad memory is in your heart.

Yes, *if it's in the well, it's coming up in the bucket."* Everyone within earshot is getting a taste of your words. Just like condemnation, un-forgiveness produces bitter water. Others, in turn, get a taste of your hurt and when they have conversations with you. Your *"reason for blame"* often becomes the topic of their discussions. The enemy has used the foothold to get in and now it becomes a snare. You find yourself keeping the pain and hurt alive and keeping the wounds fresh through your words and thoughts. It is part of your daily meditations and conversations. As others feel your anger, they actually begin to justify your un-forgiveness. This is like fertilizer nourishing and strengthening your root of bitterness.

The walls around your Lo Debar seem impenetrable, and you feel you will never get out.

Un-forgiveness also causes you to see yourself as a victim and prevents you from walking in victory. You do not see yourself as an overcomer, nor do you see yourself as adequate to stand in the face of a battle.

Just like condemnation, un-forgiveness affects many areas of your life. And left to itself, it brings destruction and opens a gateway to a long-lasting residency in Lo Debar.

When you make a willful choice to obey God and forgive the offender, you begin your journey out of your Lo Debar. **The walls will come down and you will be free.**

To extend forgiveness to the one who hurt you means you are turning them over to God. You are setting yourself free from the situation and the one who caused you pain. You will find yourself thinking about it less and less. The less you think about it the less you talk about it. The pain starts to decrease, and your healing begins when you choose to let go and forgive.

Just like condemnation that we discussed in the first week, blame can be so dangerous to the one who harbors it.

Another product of blame we must consider is self-righteousness. Blame, if left unchecked, can cause the development of a self-righteous personality. Because blame always lays the fault of what is wrong at someone else's feet, often the one blaming another will also feel entitled to pass judgement on the one they consider the perpetrator of wrong. Sometimes this can open the door to one's acquiring a judgmental condemning nature about life in general. This can cause someone to see the world through a self-righteous mindset. They truly believe their personal problems, emotional battles and even their spiritual warfare are all the fault of someone else. It is further compounded since they blame and judge others for all that is wrong in their world, and they automatically absolve themselves of any guilt or blame.

We cannot see clearly when everyone else is at fault. <u>Blame narrows our view and therefore limits our vision</u>. Everyone else is at fault; therefore, I am not to blame.

While condemnation makes you feel totally responsible, blame makes you feel everyone else is at fault. Both condemnation and blame make you feel helpless and hopeless, broken and burdened. And just as we discussed in the first week's lesson, condemnation negatively affects every area of my life.

- **My walk**
- **My worth**
- **My words**
- **My witness**
- **My worship**

These are also impacted negatively when I harbor blame.

Do you find yourself saying *(or thinking)* things like:

- *"It's all your fault."*
- *"You did this to me. You did this to us."*
- *"I'm broken and worthless because of you."*
- *"Our marriage will always suffer because of what you did."*
- *"I couldn't help what happened…but you could have."*
- *"I'm angry so much and I don't even know why."*

36

It is necessary to make the choice to forgive and put away blame. We must press forward and let go of the failures and faults of our past--both our own and those of others. Let's look at the very sound wisdom of the Apostle Paul in this familiar passage:

> Brethren, I do not count myself to have apprehended; but one thing I do, forgetting those things which are behind and reaching forward to those things which are ahead, I press toward the goal for the prize of the upward call of God in Christ Jesus (Philippians 3:13-14 NKJV).

Remember that before his conversion Paul had caused much harm and pain to many. After his conversion, he suffered greatly at the hands of many. He found it necessary to let go of both condemnation and blame and move forward in Christ. He learned the grace of Jesus Christ was sufficient, and he constantly spoke that grace over other believers. You will see this evidenced in every epistle he wrote.

And it is that same precious and sufficient grace which will enable you to lay down blame and destroy that gateway to Lo Debar.

Determine as Paul did that you must:

- *Forget those things that are in the past,*
- *Reach forward to those things ahead, and*
- *Press toward the goal.*

POINT TO PONDER

Imagine a package has been delivered to your heart's door. It is labeled **The Blame Game** on the outside. The packaging of the box is very appealing and colorful. It really is enticing. The label reads "Especially for you!" and goes on to say: "I know you are hurt and you should be. You were done so wrongly. I don't want you ever to forget how badly you have been treated; and you should never let anyone else forget either. Your heart is broken and it is not your fault."

Instructions are printed on the box that read: "Play this game for hours of endless entertainment and distraction from the real solution to the problems you are battling. **The Blame Game** is easy to play and appealing, because it absolves the players of all wrong. Hours of pleasure can be yours as you list the faults of others for everyone to know and to pass judgment on those you deem guilty, whether present or absent during the game."

You want it. Blame in the beginning makes you "feel better." It does not even matter at the moment who sent the package. Because it is so appealing, you choose to disregard the warning located in very small print on the bottom of the package! It reads *"While **The Blame Game** will bring temporary satisfaction, if blame is allowed to remain in your heart, it will grow quickly and affect all areas of your life. In the box with blame are seeds of a judgmental mindset, bitterness, un-forgiveness, and self-righteousness. These will grow rapidly. Beware: You have been warned. Sender will not take responsibility for the damage caused from using this product. Remember, we manufacture blame. We give it but we don't take it."*

Have you taken the package in? Are you battling now with blame and the pain it has caused you? Cast it away from your heart. If you have taken it in, the Lord will show you how to release it to Him through His Word.

Read and meditate on these verses:

Cast your burden on the Lord [releasing the weight of it] and He will sustain you; He will never allow the [consistently] righteous to be moved (made to slip, fall, or fail) (Psalm 55:22 AMPC).

Cast all your anxiety on him because he cares for you. Be self-controlled and alert. Your enemy the devil prowls around like a roaring lion looking for someone to devour. Resist him, standing firm in the faith, because you know that your brothers throughout the world are undergoing the same kind of sufferings. And the God of all grace, who called you to his eternal glory in Christ, after you have suffered a little while, will himself restore you and make you strong, firm and steadfast. To him be the power for ever and ever. Amen (1 Peter 5:7-11 NIV).

Write a prayer from your heart based on the instructions given in these passages:

_____

_____

_____

_____

_____

_____

When applied, these verses are truly life-changing passages. We are to cast our burdens and cares and anxiety on Him. Jesus will gladly take your burdens and set you free.

Blame is a heavy load to carry. It is a heavy "box" filled with all sorts of unpleasant items. You do not want to claim ownership of anything in that package. None of the things that come with **The Blame Game** are beneficial. Search your heart and ask yourself the question, "Have I been guilty of participating in **The Blame Game**?" Already, you know the answer. But do not pick up condemnation. Cast the blame game at the feet of Jesus.

Please cast your burden on the Lord and release the heavy weight of it. And pray for grace to not pick it back up when tempted to do so.

Release the heavy burden of blame to Him. Let go of all that comes with it. Destroy the *Blame Game Gateway* leading to Lo Debar. You will be so glad you did. You will find yourself released from the heavy burden of blame and your joy will be restored. Your journey out of Lo Debar begins with the decision to let go of blame.

Read **Romans 12:2** again at the conclusion of this week's study. Purpose in your heart that blame will not affect your mindset. Ask God daily to renew your thoughts according to His purpose for you.

> And do not be conformed to this world, but be transformed by the renewing of your mind, that you may prove what is that good and acceptable and perfect will of God (Romans 12:2 NKJV).

Read this verse and pray this prayer with the psalmist:

> Let the words of my mouth and the meditation of my heart be acceptable in Your sight, O Lord, my [firm, impenetrable] Rock and my Redeemer (Psalm 19:14 AMPC).

Make no place with your words or in your thoughts to blame others or harbor un-forgiveness.

If you battle with blaming others and the residue of hurt caused by someone else, please pray this prayer:

PRAYER

"Heavenly Father, I come before You in the precious Name of Jesus Christ. Thank You for assuring me that you will take this heavy burden of blame I have been carrying. You know I have been heartbroken over things coming my way. I am sorry for the times I

have allowed blame to become the focus of my mind. And I refuse to allow the enemy of my soul to cause me to play the blame game anymore. I want to be set free of a judgmental spirit. I do not want un-forgiveness or bitterness to take root. Uproot anything in my heart not pleasing to you. I release to You those who have hurt me. I make a choice to let go and forgive so I may walk in complete freedom and joy. Thank You, Jesus, for setting me free and for destroying the Blame Game Gateway to Lo Debar in my life."

In Jesus' name. Amen.

Take a few moments and praise God, because He has heard and answered your heart's cry.

You are free from the hurts caused by blame and un-forgiveness. He is your Healer and He will walk with you every step of the way and lead you out of Lo Debar.

Remember, the enemy is always trying to use tactics which have worked in the past. Be wise to his ways. Resist the temptation to pick up *The Blame Game*. Walk in the liberty you are given through Jesus Christ.

Stand fast therefore in the liberty by which Christ has made us free, and do not be entangled again with a yoke of bondage (Galatians 5:1, NKJV).

As you spend time journaling and in meditation this week, read again these verses:

> Brethren, I do not count myself to have apprehended; but one thing I do, forgetting those things which are behind and reaching forward to those things which are ahead, I press toward the goal for the prize of the upward call of God in Christ Jesus (Philippians 3:13-14 NKJV).

With renewed determination, I will forget those things that are in the past; forgive those who have hurt me; reach forward to those things ahead and press toward the goal.

We have talked about condemnation and blame. *It's My Fault,* and *It's Your Fault.* We discussed how those mindsets can lead us to Lo Debar. But what about the times we end up in Lo Debar, but we have no idea how or why we arrived there?

In week three we will discuss unexpected and inexplicable seasons of darkness that land us in Lo Debar.

It's Nobody's Fault so, then, how did I get here?

Week 3

POWER TRUTH

"IT'S NOBODY'S FAULT"

Our Deliverer from the Darkness of Lo Debar

This week, we will discuss the unexpected seasons of darkness caused by circumstances that come against us. We will discuss the importance of focusing on our Deliverer instead of those circumstances.

Read, meditate on and memorize these verses:

> But as for me, I will look to the Lord and confident in Him I will keep watch; I will wait with hope and expectancy for the God of my salvation; my God will hear me. Rejoice not against me, O my enemy! When I fall, I shall arise; when I sit in darkness, the Lord shall be a light to me (Micah 7:7-8 AMPC).

Make these declarations:
- I will **look** to the Lord.
- I will be **confident** in Him.
- I will **watch** for Him.
- I will **wait** with hope and expectation.

My God will hear me.

"IT'S NOBODY'S FAULT"

Our Deliverer from the Darkness of Lo Debar
2 Samuel 9:1-5

AND DAVID said, Is there still anyone left of the house of Saul to whom I may show kindness for Jonathan's sake? And of the house of Saul there was a servant whose name was Ziba. When they had called him to David, he said to him, Are you Ziba? He said, I, your servant, am he. The king said, Is there not still someone of the house of Saul to whom I may show the [unfailing, unsought, unlimited] mercy and kindness of God? Ziba replied, Jonathan has yet a son who is lame in his feet. And the king said, Where is he? Ziba replied, He is in the house of Machir son of Ammiel in Lo Debar. Then King David sent and brought him from the house of Machir son of Ammiel at Lo Debar (2 Samuel 9: 1-5 AMPC).

IN PREPARATION for this week's study, read **2 Samuel 9:1-5**. We will discover how King David remembered his covenant with Jonathan and wanted to reach out to the house of Saul *for Jonathan's sake*. This powerful story of grace and mercy unfolds as David purposefully seeks out one he may bless with the benefits of his covenant with Jonathan.

In the first two weeks, we have looked at **2 Samuel 4:4**. We discussed how easy it would have been for the nurse to step into a lifestyle of condemnation. From the same verse, we thought about the outcome for Mephibosheth and how he could have developed a mindset of blame and un-forgiveness. We discussed how they ended up in Lo Debar, a place of "no pastures—a place of desolation, a joyless, and sorrowful place of separation."

A spiritual Lo Debar is a dreaded place of darkness for the believer.

Condemnation screams, *"It's my fault we are here!"* Blame points a finger and declares, *"It's your fault!"* Though condemnation and blame are both wrong, at least they provide an explanation as to how one ends up in a place of spiritual desolation.

What about when nobody is to blame? Something seemingly "just happens" in your life that makes no sense. Now, unexpectedly, you ended up in your own spiritual Lo Debar. ***How did I get to this place of "desolation and darkness?"***

Let us take a moment and talk about you! You are faithful to God and you are committed to your family. You are a loyal friend and even actively involved in ministry. You have poured into others bound by condemnation and blame and helped them out of their difficult places. Yet, you find yourself in a spiritual dark place. You have arrived in your own personal Lo Debar--not a place you want to be. You cannot even "tell" anyone you are there. You are someone others look to for advice and guidance. How can you possibly admit you have landed in a barren place where you feel like you are experiencing no spiritual productivity, especially when you have no explanation or understanding of how you arrived there. This makes you feel isolated and alone, even with a crowd of people around you.

I can honestly share with you that I have experienced this inexplicable season of desolation and darkness. I have met many in ministry who have experienced the same. It was in one such "season" recently when the Lord reminded me He would lead me out. It is from my personal deliverance from an unexpected dark place that this week's lesson was birthed. It is from my heart that I share this with you, and I pray it makes a difference for you as it has for me.

I love the passage in **2 Samuel 9:1-5**. It is a beautiful reminder of grace and mercy bestowed upon Mephibosheth by a covenant-keeping king. You and I have a Covenant-Keeping King and He seeks us out with His amazing grace and His "new-every-morning" mercy.

HE IS OUR DELIVERER FROM DARKNESS!

Two verses of scripture have become so dear to me. God led me to them during a very difficult time in my life. I have embraced them and made them my "battle cry." When it feels like I am in a season of darkness or in spiritual warfare I go to this passage. I referenced them in *week one* of this study, and I want us to look at them again.

> But as for me, I will look to the Lord and confident in Him I will keep watch; I will wait with hope and expectancy for the God of my salvation; my God will hear me. Rejoice not against me, O my enemy! When I fall, I shall arise; when I sit in darkness, the Lord shall be a light to me (Micah 7:7-8 AMPC).

This passage reminds us of two important things: There are occasions when *we fall,* and there are times *when we sit in darkness.*

Look to the Lord! Wait with hope and expectation. Your God will hear YOU. Let your confidence be in Him and Him alone. He is your Deliverer and He will lead you out of your place of darkness.

When the Prophet Micah wrote these verses, he was living in a dark place in history. But he was empowered by the Holy Spirit and so are we. Read **Micah 3:8** as the prophet makes this powerful declaration.

> But truly I [Micah] am full of power, of the Spirit of the Lord, and of justice and might, to declare to Jacob his transgression and to Israel his sin (Micah 3:8 AMPC).

Take a moment and read **1 John 4:4.** *Write how you feel this verse relates to* **Micah 3:8**:

_____

_____

_____

_____

_____

_____

_____

Micah declares that the power of the Spirit was within him and the same power would enable him to do all he was called by God to accomplish. The same Spirit of God will enable and empower you.

Micah also gives powerful instructions in another verse.

> He has showed you, O man, what is good. And what does the Lord require of you but to do justly, and to love kindness and mercy, and to humble yourself and walk humbly with your God (Micah 6:8 AMPC).

As believers, we are to heed instructions from the Word of God and apply them to our daily lives. Micah reminds us that God has shown us "what is good." These are simple truths we know already but are so good to remember, especially in seasons of darkness.

- **Do justly.**
- **Love kindness and mercy.**
- **Walk humbly with your God.**

When we are in a place of darkness, feeling isolated and unproductive, these simple instructions will help us stay the course.

Do justly. Do not react to the situation. Emotions are elevated during trying times but we cannot let them lead us. As we have already discussed, emotions are fleeting and will cause us to react hastily and make mistakes. It is imperative to respond by seeking wisdom from the Lord, especially in stressful times.

Love kindness and mercy. Extend a Christ-like attitude toward all who are near you, even to those who may be unkind or unconcerned during your battle. Because you have ministered to others often, those in need of advice and help may likely seek you out, even in the midst of your own crisis. Usually, they are unaware that you yourself are hurting. This can actually accentuate your feelings of isolation and sorrow. But still, be careful to extend kindness and mercy. Do not let this temporary season of darkness hinder you from being His hand extended. He will bless you abundantly for your faithfulness in your times of battle.

Walk humbly with God. Rest in the assurance that you can trust Him even if you are in unchartered waters. He will guide you through this unfamiliar place, and He will never forsake you in your time of need. You may not fully understand the path you are on, but when you trust Jesus to be your Guide, the destination will be good.

It is hard to acknowledge this next statement, but it is necessary for us to consider it: If you are *not* applying these principles in your life, your actions may be the reason you are in a season of darkness.

Darkness that comes from compromise or disobedience is a different and dangerous darkness. We will discuss that kind of darkness in next week's lesson.

Take time to reevaluate your life. Determine to walk according to **Micah 6:8**! And rejoice knowing His Light will come regardless of the reason for the darkness that may surround you.

Write a heartfelt prayer asking God to help you to walk with renewed determination according to **Micah 6:8:**

_____

_____

_____

_____

_____

_____

_____

And remember, to the believer who is applying these principles and living according to them, be assured that *your darkness is temporary.*

Let's think about the verses we read and make them our determination and declaration as Micah did.

> But as for me, I will look to the Lord and confide in Him I will keep watch; I will wait with hope and expectancy for the God of my salvation; my God will hear me. Rejoice not against me, O my enemy! When I fall, I shall arise; when I sit in darkness, the Lord shall be a light to me (Micah 7:7 AMPC).

Remember, there are occasions when we fall—when we are pushed down by circumstances which can catch us off guard. Rejoice, knowing that when we fall—we SHALL get back up. This declaration can be translated simply to say that *"We are either up or getting up."* We will not stay down.

And in those unexpected seasons of darkness, the Lord shall be a light for us.

I want to share from a personal point of view for a moment. I am very close to both my sisters. I am the middle of three girls. So, I am blessed with an older and younger sister. They are both so dear to me and I cannot imagine what my life would be without them in it.

As I have been writing this study, I asked them to send me a personal note from their journals. I am sharing these with their permission and blessing. They serve as their testimonies of God's faithfulness during one of their seasons of circumstantial darkness—their time in Lo Debar.

Both of them write beautifully and they have a unique way of expressing their love for God and His faithfulness to them. Jana, my younger sister, sent a devotion she wrote when her husband had received a dreaded and fearful diagnosis. She and her family entered a season in Lo Debar because of circumstances they could not control. It was during that season of darkness that Jana penned these thoughts in the form of a devotional from **Psalm 27:5**.

HIDE ME FROM THE STORM!
By Jana K. Broome

A friend of ours so graciously offered us a week in his condo in a beautiful vacation spot for Bryan to get some doctor recommended R&R. It has been such a nice week here on the top floor of a tall condo building. Just what we needed. Just what the doctor ordered.

But, tonight as I have been trying to sleep in a strange place (which is never easy for me to do) I see a storm approaching outside the huge bedroom window. The skies are blacker than a normal night sky and the lightning is streaking across, momentarily giving enough light to show me the heavy rain that is falling. The storm seems a little scarier the higher up I am in it. Being on the 6th floor makes it seem as if the storm is more powerful to me than normal. It's like I'm on top of a high cliff with the storm striking all around me.

It sort of feels like it did back in the fall when our storm came with Bryan's sickness. We felt as if our life was going smoothly. We were on the top of the mountain. Then the winds began to blow and the storm came. And it hit us fiercely! The lightning flashed, showing us how hard the rains were falling. The winds blew all around us. And I felt afraid--for a bit.

Then, the Lord so sweetly reminded me that we were being held safely in God's Hand. He would hide me during the storm. And just like tonight, it might have seemed like I was high up and right in the middle of the storm around me. But in reality, the

Lord placed us where we were, and that was out of reach of danger.

In the *New Living Translation* in Psalm 27:5 it says, "For He will conceal me there when troubles come; He will hide me in his sanctuary. He will place me out of reach on a high rock."

See, God did not place us where we are in our trial to put us right in the middle of our storm. Instead, He placed us high on a Rock so we cannot be reached by our enemy during our storm. We have nothing to fear on this Rock while our enemy flashes and rains doubt and fear all around us. No, indeed! If our feet are firmly planted on this Rock that our Good, Good Father has placed us, we have nothing to fear. And instead of it seeming as if we are right in the middle of this storm, know that we are placed out of its reach. And we are in the perfect vantage point so we can see it around us. We can see the storm but we don't have to fear it. If we stand firmly on the Rock, Christ Jesus, we know that God is keeping us safe from it all.

So let the storms rage. Let the lightning flash and the winds blow. For I know when the storm has ended, everything will be okay. I was placed in His sanctuary. I was placed in His care. Everything will be fine when the storm passes by.

And, Praise God! Everything *was* fine when Jana's storm passed.

My oldest sister, Judy, has a gentle and sweet spirit. Everybody who knows her loves her. She is the mother of three awesome children, one who is a special needs son. It was during Judy's season in Lo-debar when her son, Jason, was so sick and in the hospital for a long extended time that she had this thought. Jason was critical and Judy was by his side when she journaled this:

FROM THE JOURNAL OF JUDY K. WHITE:
Because He bends down to listen, I will pray as long as I have breath (Psalm 116:2, NLT).

It makes me happy to know that He bends down to listen to me, like Daddy did when I was little. I knew when Daddy bent down close, I had his full attention. So I feel that when I pray, and He bends to listen, I have His full attention; and that is an amazing feeling. My Heavenly Father, who is the King of the Universe, is listening carefully to me!!! I find great comfort in knowing He loves us. Oh! How He loves us!

Judy rested in His love during her dark place.

And both my sisters *did* leave these seasons in Lo Debar. God answered their prayers. During their trials, His sufficient grace was present every moment. Yes, they were in Lo Debar, but they were never there alone.

And He will walk with you each step of the way.

Both Judy and Jana held on to the assurance of the Lord's presence, and it gave them peace and comfort during their trials.

Just as my sisters did, please take a few moments and write a verse that ministered to you during a dark place in your life:

_____

_____

_____

_____

_____

_____

_____

Let's look again to **Micah 7:7.**

We must realize the importance of Micah 7:7 and apply it accordingly before verse *("Do not rejoice over me, my enemy.")* becomes a reality. Let's look closely at the *"I wills"* found in this verse.

But as for me, I will **look** to the Lord. I will **be confident** in Him. I will **watch** for Him. I will **wait** with hope and expectation. My God will hear me.

- **I will look.**
- **I will be confident.**
- **I will watch.**
- **I will wait.**

In this verse there are two more very important words that we need to discuss: **Hope** and **expectation**.

I believe it is important to note that Micah said he will wait "with hope."

Hope is something a believer does **(Psalm 119:147),** and hope is something a believer has. Either way you use it, "hope" is a powerful word. We have hope because Our God will hear and deliverer us. We are not silently hoping without assurance. For many believers, the noun form of *hope* may be more assuring than the verb form of *hope*. Either way hope is a precious possession given to us by God.

Another important word is "expectation." Waiting is not something some of us enjoy. But if we wait with *expectation* we can be patient. Expectation creates anticipation. Anticipation keeps you alert and watchful. Expect His mercy and kindness to find you, just like it found Mephibosheth. David was a king but also a man who kept his covenant. We serve a Covenant-Keeping God; and He will make Himself known and be light in your darkness.

The darkness caused by unexpected circumstances sometimes bombarding the believer is not the same darkness the world is in. The darkness of a sinful, unredeemed life is permanent, unless Jesus is received and salvation is experienced. The darkness can invade the life of a believer unexpectedly and sometimes inexplicably. Yet, in Jesus darkness is always *temporary*.

Remember we are called OUT of darkness into His marvelous light.

> But you are a chosen race, a royal priesthood, a dedicated nation, [God's] own purchased, special people, that you may set forth the wonderful deeds and display the virtues and perfections of Him Who called you out of darkness into His marvelous light (1 Peter 2:9 AMPC).

Yes, the darkness that invades the life of a believer is often circumstantial. With Jesus, it is TEMPORARY. Such darkness can be brought on by battles we face; spiritually, emotionally, physically or even financially. Situations of sorrow and sickness that causing you pain, and/or affecting someone you love and care for can distract and cause darkness to overshadow you. These trials can cause darkness to invade our space and make us feel isolated and unproductive. These unexpected events can cause us to end up in Lo Debar but only for a season. *We are just passing through.*

This kind of darkness can be misleading and deceptive. The definition of darkness is simply *"the absence of light."* So, darkness does not and cannot exist in the presence of light. Light always dispels it.

I must stress this again! This kind of darkness for the believer in Jesus is temporary. And we MUST see it that way.

Read this familiar verse again:

> For His anger is but for a moment, His favor is for life; Weeping may endure for a night, But joy comes in the morning (Psalm 30:5, NKJV).

Whatever situation, sorrow or sickness having caused you to feel like you are in a place of no pastures, no harvest, desolation and joyless; please know your weeping is not going to last. **Joy is on the way!**

Do not be afraid. God will invade your darkness. He will speak light into your situation.

Let's read another familiar passage.

> In the beginning God (prepared, formed, fashioned, and) created the heavens and the earth. The earth was without form and an empty waste, and darkness was upon the face of the very great deep. The Spirit of God was moving (hovering, brooding) over the face of the waters. And God said, Let there be light; and there was light (Genesis 1:1-3 AMPC).

The Spirit of God was moving, hovering, brooding over the darkness, confusion and void. And when it was in His timing for the darkness to end, He spoke, *"Let there be light; and there was light."* He made something beautiful out of what once was emptiness and darkness. He will do the same for you.

God knows exactly where you are and He is close to you, especially in your dark places. He is carefully watching over you. He is going to speak and light will come. This darkness—this season in Lo Debar—is temporary. You will produce a harvest. You will see your prayers answered. God will create something beautiful in you and through you. Look with confidence to Him. Wait with hope and expectation. God will not disappoint you. You will not reside in Lo Debar forever.

Nevertheless, be warned; the enemy never plays fair. When we are in our season of darkness, the enemy fabricates what is going on around us. He shows us a long list of things with us "in the room." If we focus on our fears, we begin to imagine what he is saying to us. Remember, your imagination is powerful, and those fears begin to take on life. Remember as kids, how we always told ghost stories in the dark? Haunted houses always have the lights out. There is always a monster under the bed.

Darkness can cause us to focus on the unknown--the "what ifs." If we listen to the fabrications of the enemy fear can set in, and we may begin developing faith in the wrong kingdom.

Instead of focusing on *"what if"*—focus on *"He will."*

My God will hear me. I will see Him bring light to my darkness. This too shall pass. I will not reside in Lo Debar. **I am just passing through.**

POINTS TO PONDER

When our children are young, we usually develop a routine that works well for them when we are putting them down to rest at night. When our sons were small, they liked bedtime stories and I loved reading to them. Now, I look forward to that same opportunity with our first grandson. As a new grandmother, I love it when I can cuddle with little Josiah and read to him at bedtime. Then, when he falls asleep, I will carefully place him in his crib. The lights are already dimmed but when he is sleeping soundly, we turn them out so that he can rest peacefully. Emily, his beautiful mom, knows just what is best for him when he is down for the night. Darkness prevents any distractions should he awaken. If Josiah does wake up crying or restless before morning, his mom or dad will go in his room and stand by his crib. They will sweetly talk to him, sing to him, and touch him to soothe and assure him of their presence. *They do not turn the light on just yet.* The light comes later after Josiah has had adequate rest.

You see, during the "season of darkness" we must be still and wait with hope and expectation. Instead of becoming impatient or stressful, we can rest knowing God is there and He is working all things for our good. Yes! What the enemy means for harm, God will use for your good. We can actually find rest in the darkness when we are fully aware His light is coming. Listen in your season of darkness. Be still and you will sense His presence and feel His touch as He assuring you He is close by. Instead of allowing the darkness to cause fear of the unknown, REST, knowing God is working on your behalf and that the light is coming at the right moment.

Look at this beautiful and comforting verse of Scripture.

> The Lord your God in your midst, The Mighty One, will save; He will rejoice over you with gladness, He will quiet you with His love, He will rejoice over you with singing (Zephaniah 3:17 NKJV).

This promises The Lord to be in your midst, rejoicing over you. He will quiet you with His love. When you are feeling like the darkness is too long and overwhelming, listen with your heart.

His love is present to quiet you and bring you comfort. He is assuring you of His presence in your season of darkness. He is singing a sweet song of love over you.

Let's read the same verse in the *Amplified Version.*

> The Lord your God is in the midst of you, a Mighty One, a Savior [Who saves]! He will rejoice over you with joy; He will rest [in silent satisfaction] and in His love He will be silent and make no mention [of past sins, or even recall them]; He will exult over you with singing (Zephaniah 3:17 AMPC).

This reminds us that God will make no mention of your past sins or failures or even recall them.

Take comfort in this promise and, in your darkness, let it destroy the lies and accusations with which the enemy desires to assault you.

Pause and take a minute to reflect. Then, write a prayer of gratitude to God for being so near when you are in a season of darkness. Praise Him in this prayer from a thankful heart for His loving care.

_____

_____

_____

_____

_____

_____

_____

Rest! God has got you. This too shall pass.

I will rest in this season. What the enemy intended to hurt me, God will use for my good.

> And we know that all things work together for good to those who love God, to those who are the called according to His purpose (Romans 8:28 NKJV).

THE LIGHT REVEALS TRUTH in my darkness.

I must read the Word I must worship in the dark place. When I do, it shifts my focus from the darkness to the Deliverer from Darkness. My fears diminish, and my faith increases.

Who is my Deliverer?

> Then Jesus spoke to them again, saying, 'I am the light of the world. He who follows Me shall not walk in darkness, but have the light of life (John 8:12 NKJV).

You are following Him. You shall not walk in endless darkness. Remember, this darkness is temporary. He will be the light that illuminates your darkness, and He will lead you out of Lo Debar.

When the light comes, you will realize He has given you treasures in the time of darkness. He is mindful of your faithfulness to Him in your time of darkness and desolation. He will bless you and give you hidden riches of secret places.

Wait with hope and expectancy. You will not be disappointed.

And I will give you the treasures of darkness and hidden riches of secret places, that you may know that it is I, the Lord, the God of Israel, Who calls you by your name (Isaiah 45:3 AMPC).

He will strengthen you and remind you of your purpose and His plan for your life. The best is ahead. The darkness is temporary. It is an illusion that cannot exist in the presence of His Light.

The LIGHT IS COMING! This season in Lo Debar is nearing its end.

Joy is on its way.

Memorize and journal these verses. Hold tightly to the comforting truth found in them.

But as for me, I will look to the Lord and confident in Him I will keep watch; I will wait with hope and expectancy for the God of my salvation; my God will hear me. Rejoice not against me, O my enemy! When I fall, I shall arise; when I sit in darkness, the Lord shall be a light to me (Micah 7:7-8 NKJV).

If you have found yourself in an unexpected, or an inexplicable season in the darkness of Lo Debar,

PRAY THIS PRAYER

"God I come before You in the precious Name of Jesus, My Light and My salvation. Jesus, I trust You. I don't always understand this

journey and the places I sometimes find myself. But I am determined to trust and hold tightly to your Word. I will look to You, Lord. I will remain confident in You! I will watch. I will wait with hope and expectation. You are hearing me. When I fall, I will arise. I am either up or getting up, but I will not stay down. This darkness is temporary. What the enemy meant for harm, You will turn for my good. I will rest in complete confidence, fully assured of Your Presence. The Light is coming. The darkness will be dispelled. This season in Lo Debar is temporary. Thank You, Lord, for the treasures You are laying up for me even in the season of darkness. I praise You and I am anticipating great things just ahead. I rejoice because You are faithful and Your word is truth! I find rest and peace in that assurance."

In Jesus' name, Amen.

- **I will look.**
- **I will be confident.**
- **I will watch.**
- **I will wait.**
- **For My God is hearing me.**

Take a few moments and praise Him from your heart in complete confidence and assurance that He hears you when you pray. Spend time journaling, as my sisters did. As you write, think of the faithfulness of God during your trials.

> THE LORD is my Light and my Salvation--whom shall I fear or dread? The Lord is the Refuge and Stronghold of my life--of whom shall I be afraid? (Psalm 27:1 AMPC).

In next week's lesson, we will look at a different kind of darkness, occurring as the result of wrong thinking and living a "Life in Lo Debar." We will talk about how we are to guard our minds against receiving the lies of the enemy and against "dimming the light" of truth in our heart.

We will discuss darkness caused by compromise when we settle in Lo Debar.

As you study and meditate this week, instead of focusing on "what if," focus on "He will."

Wait with hope and expectancy. You will not be disappointed!

Week 4

POWER TRUTH

MY MENTALITY BECOMES MY REALITY

Life in Lo Debar

The enemy wants us to imagine the worst He wants us to see all of us defeated and helpless. He wants to give us thoughts that cause us to compromise and dim the light of truth.

> For though we walk in the flesh, we do not war after the flesh: (For the weapons of our warfare are not carnal, but mighty through God to the pulling down of strongholds;) Casting down imaginations, and every high thing that exalteth itself against the knowledge of God, and bringing into captivity every thought to the obedience of Christ (2 Corinthians 10:3-5 KJV).

We must heed the instructions given in 2 Corinthians 10:3-5:

- **Cast down ungodly, negative imaginations.**
- **Dismiss and denounce every high thing and every thought that exalts itself against the knowledge of Our God.**
- **We must bring every thought into alignment with the Word of God and to the obedience of Christ.**

Pray and ask God to help you apply the instructions given in this passage. Journal and meditate on the powerful information of these verses.

Week 4

MY MENTALITY BECOMES MY REALITY

Life in Lo Debar
2 Samuel 9:1-5

Then King David sent and brought him from the house of Machir son of Ammiel at Lo Debar. And Mephibosheth son of Jonathan, the son of Saul, came to David and fell on his face and did obeisance. David said, Mephibosheth! And he answered, Behold your servant! David said to him, Fear not, for I will surely show you kindness for Jonathan your father's sake, and will restore to you all the land of Saul your father [grandfather], and you shall eat at my table always. And [the cripple] bowed himself and said, What is your servant, that you should look upon such a dead dog as I am? (2 Samuel 9:5-8 NKJV).

I N THE FIRST THREE weeks of this study, we have been looking into scenarios that could lead us to Lo Debar. This week we want to look deeper into the hurtful effects of "living and settling in" and what happens when we compromise, adapt and accept a mindset that is produced from a negative atmosphere.

Read again **2 Samuel 9:8**. At this point in the story, Mephibosheth has been summoned and brought out of Lo Debar and is now in the presence of King David. But we read in Mephibosheth's response the negativity he feels about himself.

When King David addresses Mephibosheth and assures him of the blessings he will provide because of the covenant with Jonathan; Mephibosheth's response is heartbreaking. In one question to King David, Mephibosheth's brokenness and total lack of self-worth are clearly revealed.

What is your servant, that you should look upon such a dead dog as I am (2 Samuel 9:8 NKJV)?

Mephibosheth is out of Lo Debar, but Lo Debar is not out of him.

Mephibosheth had likely heard most of his life so much negativity about his brokenness. A list of what *could have* and *should have* happened in his life was constantly in the forefront of his mind.

His physical and emotional pain assaulted him daily. As we discussed in the second week of this study, he could have developed a bitter, unforgiving spirit. It is apparent is his question to King David, that his self-loathing was overwhelming.

"Why would you even look at me? I am nothing more than a dead dog!"

Mephibosheth apparently had rehearsed all the negative statements and thoughts for so long until he truly believed he was worthless. His mentality was molded by what he had heard and said about himself. Even after ***his atmosphere*** and environment changed, in the very presence of the welcoming king, he still saw himself as less than nothing. His mind was shrouded in darkness.

And Mephibosheth had grown accustomed to the darkness in Lo Debar. That same darkness had invaded his mind and heart. He was no longer there physically, but his heart was formed in that environment. Darkness, despondency and depression had become his reality.

We must guard our hearts and minds. We must not speak death and discouragement over ourselves. Why is this so important? **My mentality becomes my reality.**

If I believe I am a failure, I will never attempt to succeed. If I believe I can't, I won't. If I believe it's impossible to change; change will never come. And if I believe change will never come, I begin to compromise and settle in Lo Debar.

Lo Debar now feels permanent, and darkness permeates my mind and heart.

In the first week of the study, we talked about how our mindset affected every area of our lives.

Reflect again on the list we discussed. It is so important to remember that my thoughts affect:

- **My Walk**
- **My Worth**
- **My Words**
- **My Witness**
- **My Worship**

The arrival to this place of despondency and darkness did not happen overnight with Mephibosheth. It was a process. And it was a process that began with a thought. He imagined the worst and the worst was what he got. Ultimately, he saw himself as useless and worthless as "a dead dog!"

We discussed in the first week of the study, the power of our imagination. Let's take a moment and review what we talked about.

Remember, when speculation and imagination take over in negative ways, we begin to allow the worst scenarios to unfold in our minds.

God gave us our imaginations to use in good ways. He has given us the ability to be creative and to accomplish so many things, and creativity first begins with an imaginary thought.

God desires for your imagination to give birth to creativity. The devil wants your imagination to birth condemnation, destruction and darkness, inhibiting you from walking in the path God has put before you.

We must purposefully dismiss the "worst case scenario" the enemy presents and begin to imagine the best. We must see past the moment we are in to where the Word promises we will arrive. When we shift our focus from the battle to the promises of victory, peace begins to take charge in our mind and darkness fades in the light of His truth.

The enemy wants you to be shrouded in hopelessness and darkness, but God wants you to walk in the light of His glorious truth.

Let's read this passage again:

For though we walk in the flesh, we do not war after the flesh: (For the weapons of our warfare are not carnal, but mighty through God to the pulling down of strongholds;) Casting down imaginations, and every high thing that exalteth itself against the knowledge of God, and bringing into captivity every thought to the obedience of Christ (2 Corinthians 10:3-5 KJV).

In your own words, express your thoughts on why you feel these verses are important for a healthy mindset:

_____

_____

_____

_____

_____

_____

As believers in Jesus Christ, we must remember always that our warfare is not to be fought with carnal weapons. The spiritual weapons we have been given are powerful. They are mighty and are able to pull down strongholds. We are to follow the instructions in this passage in order to stop the plot of the enemy against our thought life.

We must do the following:

- *Cast down ungodly, negative imaginations.*
- *Dismiss and denounce every high thing and every thought that exalts itself against the knowledge of Our God.*
- *Bring every thought into alignment with the Word of God and to the obedience of Christ.*

Based on the instructions given in these verses, we can expect Satan to tempt us with ungodly and negative imaginations. We know that he will attempt to give us thoughts to undermine and alter the truth about God, His love and power that work in us. We must dismiss and discredit the lies of the enemy, or he will construct a stronghold one thought at a time, putting us in the darkness of Lo Debar.

> Be sober, be vigilant; because your adversary the devil walks about like a roaring lion, seeking whom he may devour. Resist him, steadfast in the faith, knowing that the same sufferings are experienced by your brotherhood in the world. But may the God of all grace, who called us to His eternal glory by Christ Jesus, after you have suffered a while, perfect, establish, strengthen, and settle you (1 Peter 5:8-10 NKJV).

71

Read this passage in 1 Peter 5. List the instructions given as you read over the passage carefully:

_____

_____

_____

_____

_____

_____

The *Amplified Version* says we are to "withstand him; be firm in faith against his onset—rooted, established, strong, immovable, and determined," meaning we are to be sober minded; vigilant and cautious at ALL times. We are to be firm in our faith--rooted, established, strong, immovable and determined. This describes a mindset that will produce light even in midst of great darkness.

As a follower of Christ, we must continue to be aware of the enemy's plot against us. He wants you to imagine the worst and have "faith in your fears." He wants you to live in dread, sorrow and darkness, undermining your effectiveness and your influence as a Christian disciple.

Last week we read the definition of darkness which is simply the **absence of light.**

This week, we will discuss the importance of dispelling the darkness and seeing clearly again according to the light of His truth.

As a believer, we must always be mindful that we disciple others according to the way *we* live. All of us have someone who is "watching" to see how we respond, and we lead more by our actions than we sometimes realize. Yes, by our example, in word and deed, we teach others how to live for Christ.

The enemy delights in planting seeds of doubt in the mind of a believer. He wants the light of truth to be diminished because of unbelief. As stated in **2 Corinthians 3:5,** once a negative thought contrary to the true knowledge of God exalts itself in your mind; if you are not careful, you may allow a detrimental mindset to take root. Such a mindset will then begin to diminish our faith in areas where we once stood strong.

The enemy does not want you to just doubt yourself. He wants you to doubt God.

We must be on guard to the enemy's schemes at all times. He has learned how to effectively "dim the light" in our mind.

> Keep and guard your heart with all vigilance and above all that you guard, for out of it flow the springs of life (Proverbs 4: 23, AMPC).

If we are living in areas of darkness or in places the light has grown dim, we may by example be unintentionally leading for others to do the same. If I have settled in Lo Debar, then those I disciple will too.

In week three of the study, we talked about seasons of darkness that are brought on by various circumstances we face: painful situations, sickness or sorrows, either our own or those of someone we love. These are trials that come against us in this life. Circumstantial darkness is temporary for the believer and usually comes not based on anything we do or cause.

There is a different and dangerous darkness that we must diligently guard against. This is the darkness caused by compromise.

Look again at **1 Peter 2:9.** We are called out of darkness into His marvelous light. We must not step back into the shadows of darkness by accepting the lies of the enemy. We cannot accept a thought or "doctrine" that exalts itself against the true knowledge of God. Doing so initiates the development of a destructive mindset.

> But you are a chosen race, a royal priesthood, a dedicated nation, [God's] own purchased, special people, that you may set forth the wonderful deeds and display the virtues and perfections of Him Who called you out of darkness into His marvelous light (1 Peter 2:9 AMPC).

What do you think it means to be called out of darkness?

In another powerful passage in John 12, Jesus warned against stepping back into darkness. He instructed those with Him to walk in the light of truth, even after The Light (speaking of Himself) would be gone from their presence. He encouraged them to believe in the Light, to have faith in Him and be filled with the truth the Light had brought.

> So Jesus said to them, You will have the Light only a little while longer. Walk while you have the Light [keep on living by it], so that darkness may not overtake and overcome you. He who walks about in the dark does not know where he goes [he is drifting]. While you have the Light, believe in the Light [have faith in it, hold to it, rely on it], that you may become sons of the Light and be filled with Light. Jesus said these things, and then He went away and hid Himself from them [was lost to their view] (John 12:35-36 AMPC).

The enemy knows that once a believer has seen "the light" of Jesus Christ and experienced the glorious transformation that comes with salvation from accepting Him as Lord; he has to be cunningly deceptive to pull us away from the revelation we have received.

There are so many "winds of doctrine" today! Some churches say they teach Christian doctrine. Yet, they water down truth and their doctrine actually exalts itself against the true knowledge of God.

The Word in **Ephesians 4:11-16** presents to us the necessity and purpose of the five-fold ministry. We are to preach and teach the Word of God "for the equipping of the saints," so that we all come to a greater faith in Christ; to not be swayed by every wind of doctrine that blows across our land.

If we receive less that the real truth about Jesus Christ, we may be depriving our minds of the glorious light we could receive through genuine revelation of Him. If we continue in that path, we may find ourselves tossed about with the possibility of landing in the dangerous, deceptive darkness of Lo Debar.

Read **Ephesians 4:11-16:**

> And He Himself gave some to be apostles, some prophets, some evangelists, and some pastors and teachers, for the equipping of the saints for the work of ministry, for the edifying of the body of Christ, till we all come to the unity of the faith and of the knowledge of the Son of God, to a perfect man, to the measure of the stature of the fullness of Christ; that we should no longer be children, tossed to and fro and carried about with every wind of doctrine, by the trickery of men, in the cunning craftiness of deceitful plotting, but, speaking the truth in love, may grow up in all things into Him who is the head—Christ —from whom the whole body, joined and knit together by what every joint supplies, according to the effective working by which every part does its share, causes growth of the body for the edifying of itself in love (Ephesians 4: 11-16 NKJV).

The importance of congregating where the absolute truth is taught and presented by anointed men and women of the five-fold ministry cannot be overstated.

If you are called in ministry to one of these vital areas of service, you are *responsible* to equip people with the genuine, absolute, God-given, Word-based, redemptive, revelation truth and knowledge of Jesus Christ. ***Anything less dims the light.***

Reading **Proverbs 29:18** reminds us that without a vision defined as *"a redemptive, revelation of God,"* people cast off restraint. Without divine revelation, they have no reasoning, or understanding to enable them to live in the light of truth. But once someone receives revelation and accepts truth, the light of truth dispels darkness and changes everything. **All things become new!**

So, through negative thoughts, weakened or altered pure biblical doctrine, the enemy begins to attempt to weaken and alter our revelation of God that may lead to ***compromise.*** And a life of compromise will cause the light to dim.

Where there is no revelation, the people cast off restraint; But happy is he who keeps the law (Proverbs 29:18, NKJV).

> Where there is no vision [no redemptive revelation of God], the people perish; but he who keeps the law [of God, which includes that of man]—blessed (happy, fortunate, and enviable) is he (Proverbs 29:18 AMPC).

Remember, the enemy desires to come at us with one negative thought at a time. If we entertain negative thinking, he continues to build upon them. If we do not stop the process, he is able to construct a stronghold in our mind; a place of darkness; our own personal Lo Debar. And spiritually, we begin to unwittingly "dim the light' in our heart, seeing ourselves in a "different and dimmed light" than God intended. It is the enemy's ultimate intent is to do the same with our view of God.

We must be so careful not to allow our mentality will ultimately become our reality.

POINTS TO PONDER

Not long ago, I had come home from a conference, and I found my husband doing some helpful things around the house. This is always a blessing and I greatly appreciate it. One of the things he had done was change the lightbulb in the hallway of our home. When I turned the light on I was shocked at what I saw. We really needed to paint the hallway walls. And I had not even realized it. Why? Because the bulb he had replaced had a much lower wattage. During the time the bulb was out of commission, the hallway had a short span of time with no light at all. So the hallway had gradually gone from dim to dark.

I would be home only a couple of days before traveling again, and this time my husband was able to travel with me. So neither of us had time to paint. I looked at him and laughingly said, "We either need to go get a lower watt light bulb or buy paint." So off to the local home goods store we went to buy a weaker bulb. The lower wattage helped obscure the areas that needed change in the hallway until we had a more convenient time to 'fix the problem."

I am old enough to remember when buying a light bulb was not a major undertaking. You just ran into the store, grabbed the wattage you needed and that was that--but not anymore. Now, bulbs are LED (light emitting diode), CFL (compact fluorescent), Incandescent, Halogen, etc. The lighting section actually provides light bulb buying guides so you can choose the correct bulb and wattage to meet your needs and preferences. Also there are some stores displaying the lights so you can determine which light flatters your skin tone or wall paint color the best. You can look at your reflection or hold your paint sample card next to the light and make your choice. What? I had no idea how complicated buying had gotten.

Nevertheless, we finally chose the bulb we thought would adequately camouflage the many imperfections in the hallway wall until we had time to deal with it.

As we were leaving the store, I felt as if the Lord spoke to my heart and said, "That is the way some people are choosing churches these days." I felt grief overwhelm me as I pondered what I heard in my heart.

Are we choosing churches that simply suit our lifestyle and choices? Is our preference to congregate in places where the real and difficult problems we face are not addressed? Are we putting off dealing with our issues until a more convenient time? Worse! Are we purposefully selecting places of worship, through compromise, to dim the light of truth, creating doctrines that deny the need for change?

Let's be honest, it's easier to change the light bulb than to paint.

Discipleship is work. It requires time and effort to disciple a new convert. We can never get so busy, even in our work "for God," to choose to "lower the light" until a more convenient time; either in self-evaluation or mentoring a young disciple.

The danger is real. If we stay too long in a dimmed light, we find ourselves adjusting to the darkness.

- Adjusting to the dark leads to compromise.
- Compromise leads to complacency.
- And complacency gives way to a carnal mind.

Compromise means "to make ***concessions.***

Complacency means "to have a feeling of quiet pleasure or security, often while unaware of some potential danger." It means "to be satisfied or settle for an existing situation."

Think about this. In the seasons of darkness caused by circumstances, the enemy wants us to fear the unknown. He wants to destroy our faith through fear. He does not want us to believe God can or will bring us out.

But in darkness caused by willful ***compromise*** on our part, Satan's design is for us to feel secure. He wants us to settle in and dwell in Lo Debar. Because in the darkness of compromise, we tend to make ***concessions*** to him. Perhaps they are small concessions at first, but then the concessions become more frequent and in more areas. Afterward, we find ourselves stepping into complacency; settling for an existing situation. We settle for so much less that God ever intended.

And sadly, by example, we lead others to do the same.

Look at the contrast. God wants us to rest in Him during warfare and ***circumstantial darkness***. He desires for us to be reassured and know He is both able and willing to bring us out victoriously. He wants us to be confident that He WILL bring light to our darkness. God wants our faith to increase as a result of another victory won through Him.

He prefers our being very uncomfortable in seasons of darkness caused by compromise.

We are not meant to live in the darkness of Lo Debar caused by compromise that leads to complacency. We are not to take up residency there.

We are not to build our churches in the land of compromise. We are never to be or produce complacent disciples. If we do, we continually find ourselves conceding to less than God has purposed for us and empowered us to accomplish. When we live continually in an atmosphere of dimmed light we grow accustomed to the dark. This can become the new norm.

For those who live according to the flesh set their minds on the things of the flesh, but those who live according to the Spirit, the things of the Spirit. For to be carnally minded is death, but to be spiritually minded is life and peace. Because the carnal mind is enmity against God; for it is not subject to the law of God, nor indeed can be. So then, those who are in the flesh cannot please God (Romans 8:5-8 NKJV).

Lo Debar—that place of "no pastures and desolation and darkness" is no place for the believer to live.

- **Are we settling and willfully congregating in Lo Debar?**
- **Have we become accustomed to the dimming light?**
- **Are we compromising doctrinal truths we once held dear?**
- **As a result, are we surrendering the genuine and unchanging redemptive revelation of Christ?**
- **Do we "look better" spiritually when the light is dim?**

We must guard our hearts according to Jesus' warning in **John 12: 35-36**, when He addressed the believers. Jesus said that we not let darkness "overtake and overcome" us. Dimming the light is a gradual process causing one to drift aimlessly, eventually finding himself walking about in darkness not knowing where he will end up.

Remember, we must be on constant guard against the enemy's schemes! Let's read this verse in Proverbs again:

Keep and guard your heart with all vigilance and above all that you guard, for out of it flow the springs of life (Proverbs 4:23 AMPC).

Write a prayer from your heart asking God to help you keep guard over your heart!

Above all the things we protect and keep, we must guard our hearts from thoughts that contradict the Word. We cannot allow the enemy to dim the light of truth through compromise. The effects of compromise can be devastating--not only to us but to those we lead and instruct.

We must daily fill our hearts with truth. Truth will set you apart for His service. It will keep the light shining brightly in your heart, and it allows no room for compromise.

Jesus was so aware that the enemy would attempt to deceive through compromising the truth. After all, that was a plot that worked effectively with Adam and Eve in the Garden of Eden. So, Jesus prayed this beautiful prayer for you.

> Sanctify them by Your truth. Your word is truth. As You sent Me into the world, I also have sent them into the world. And for their sakes I sanctify Myself, that they also may be sanctified by the truth (John 17:17 NKJV).

Read these verses and, like the psalmist, make them your prayer.

> Let the words of my mouth and the meditation of my heart Be acceptable in Your sight, O Lord, my strength and my Redeemer (Psalm 19:14 NKJV).

81

Look deep into my heart, God, and find out everything I am thinking. Don't let me follow evil ways, but lead me in the way that time has proven true (Psalm 139:23-24 CEV).

Fear, uncertainty and the lack of peace always come from thoughts the enemy gives.

For God has not given us a spirit of fear, but of power and of love and of a sound mind (2 Timothy 1:7, NKJV).

Read this verse and remember we are to let the peace of God "rule" in our hearts.

And let the peace of God rule in your hearts, to which also you were called in one body; and be thankful (Colossians 3:15, NKJV).

Let's also read it in the *Amplified Version* for further clarity.

And let the peace (soul harmony which comes) from Christ rule (act as umpire continually) in your hearts [deciding and settling with finality all questions that arise in your minds, in that peaceful state] to which as [members of Christ's] one body you were also called [to live]. And be thankful (appreciative), [giving praise to God always] (Colossians 3:15 AMPC).

This powerful verse of instruction tells us what we should do.

Let the peace of God rule (umpire) our thoughts. If a thought enters your mind contradicting the peace that comes through Christ and the promises of His Word, dismiss it. Reject it. Like an umpire making the call, be bold in letting peace declare negative thoughts "out" of your mind.

Read **John 14:27**. *Express what this verse means to you in connection with* **Colossians 3:15**:

_____

_____

_____

82

Settle the questions that arise in your mind. Look beyond the battle to the impending victory promised by your Covenant-Keeping King. Do not let the enemy dim the light of truth in your heart. Do not allow him to bring imaginations that delude the power of God. Regarding the true nature and character God, do not allow him to create questions that lead to compromise.

Always remember we are called to live in His perfect peace. His peace is not to be determined by circumstances that come and go. His peace is perfect and passes all understanding. When we abide in His peace, and make no room for compromise, the enemy cannot dim the light.

Be thankful. A heart that has confidence in God maintains an attitude of gratitude. How? Because you wait with "hope and expectation," fully assured He will provide light in your darkness.

Mephibosheth is an example of one who allowed his mind to be conformed to his environment. He had adjusted to the darkness of his situations. He had allowed darkness to overtake and overcome him.

Mephibosheth suffered from both circumstantial darkness and spiritual darkness. He needed deliverance. And, praise God, deliverance came in the form of a covenant-keeping king. Your deliverance will come, regardless of the reasons for your darkness.

I will not settle in the darkness of compromise. I will not concede to the enemy's plot to cause me to settle in Lo Debar. I will not see God for less than who He is in me and for me. I will no longer see myself as less than He created me to be.

83

The same God who brings me out of darkness caused by circumstances will bring me out of darkness caused by compromise.

Let's read our battle cry again!

But as for me, I will look to the Lord and confident in Him I will keep watch; I will wait with hope and expectancy for the God of my salvation; my God will hear me. Rejoice not against me, O my enemy! When I fall, I shall arise; when I sit in darkness, the Lord shall be a light to me (Micah 7:7-8 AMPC).

- **I will look.**
- **I will be confident.**
- **I will watch.**
- **I will wait.**
- **For My God is hearing me.**

I will not settle in Lo Debar!

Take a moment and make this your sincere heart's prayer.

PRAYER

"Heavenly Father, I come to You in the Precious and Powerful Name of Jesus. I praise you for your Word, for Your Word is truth. Sanctify me and set me apart daily for Your service through Your Word as it resides in me. Forgive me for the times I may have compromised unwittingly or knowingly to the plot of the enemy. Help me to guard my heart continually against ungodly thoughts that may lead me to compromise and complacency. Thank You for Your promise to lead and guide me into all truth. Help me to hunger and thirst daily for more of Your Word. For the Living Bread will fill my mind; and I will not receive any thought that exalts itself against the knowledge of My God. My mind will not be conformed to this world or alter because situations I may face. Help me to walk in your wisdom daily and

instruct others by my example to do the same. With Your sufficient grace, I will not dim the light of truth or live a life of compromise."
In Jesus' name. Amen.

As you spend time in prayer and journaling this week, read and meditate further on this passage:

> Look deep into my heart, God, and find out everything I am thinking. Don't let me follow evil ways, but lead me in the way that time has proven true (Psalm 139:23-24 CEV).

Next week we will look at Our Covenant-Keeping King. Who is this King of Glory?

POWER TRUTH

THE COVENANT-KEEPING KING

The Great Grace Getaway from Lo Debar

In **Matthew 16:13-19**, Jesus was talking with those closest to Him, and He wanted to hear their response to perhaps the most important question ever asked, ***But who do you say that I am (Matthew 16: 15 NKJV)?***

Peter's response is recorded in verse 16:

Simon Peter answered and said, "'You are the Christ, the Son of the living God" (Matthew 16:16, NKJV).

We must walk in the revelation of that truth. So as you study this week, meditate on the magnitude of Peter's response. Take time to praise the Lord for providing His sufficient grace and our way out of Lo Debar. Pray and ask for greater revelation of Our Covenant-Keeping King.

THE COVENANT- KEEPING KING

The Great Grace Getaway from Lo Debar
2 Samuel 9:1-11

NOW DAVID SAID, "Is there still anyone who is left of the house of Saul, that I may show him kindness for Jonathan's sake?" And there was a servant of the house of Saul whose name was Ziba. So when they had called him to David, the king said to him, "Are you Ziba?" He said, "At your service!" Then the king said, "Is there not still someone of the house of Saul, to whom I may show the kindness of God?" And Ziba said to the king, "There is still a son of Jonathan who is lame in his feet." So the king said to him, "Where is he?" And Ziba said to the king, "Indeed he is in the house of Machir the son of Ammiel, in Lo Debar." Then King David sent and brought him out of the house of Machir the son of Ammiel, from Lo Debar. Now when Mephibosheth the son of Jonathan, the son of Saul, had come to David, he fell on his face and prostrated himself. Then David said, "Mephibosheth?" And he answered, "Here is your servant!" So David said to him, "Do not fear, for I will surely show you kindness for Jonathan your father's sake, and will restore to you all the land of Saul your grandfather; and you shall eat bread at my table continually." Then he bowed himself, and said, "What is your servant, that you should look upon such a dead dog as I?" And the king called to Ziba, Saul's servant, and said to him, "I have given to your master's son all that belonged to Saul and to all his house. You therefore, and your sons and your servants, shall work the land for him, and you shall bring in the harvest, that your master's son may have food to eat. But Mephibosheth your master's son shall eat bread at my table always." Now Ziba had fifteen sons and twenty servants. Then Ziba said to the king, "According to all that my lord the king has commanded his servant, so will your servant do." "As for Mephibosheth," said the king, "he shall eat at my table like one of the king's sons (2 Samuel 9:1-11 NKJV).

IN THE FIRST four weeks of our study, we looked at this passage of scripture and discussed the factors leading to a life in Lo Debar. Also we considered the negative effects of time spent in our own spiritual Lo Debar.

This week, we will look closely at our Deliverer—Our Covenant-Keeping King.

Read **2 Samuel 9:1-11** again; and this time, make King David your focus.

Notice as you read that David:

- **Remembered his covenant of grace and mercy, vs. 1;**
- **Sought Mephibosheth out, vs. 3;**
- **Brought him out of Lo Debar—that place of desolation, vs. 5;**
- **Spoke peace over him when Mephibosheth was afraid, vs. 7;**
- **Looked beyond his faults (low self-worth) and brokenness, vs. 8;**
- **Provided for all his present and future needs, vs. 9;**

- **Covered him with <u>grace and mercy</u> and made a place for him permanently at his table, vs. 10;**
- **<u>Made him as one of his sons</u>, vs. 11.**

When you read all King David did for Mephibosheth, how do you see the story in comparison to <u>what Jesus did for you?</u>

_____

_____

_____

_____

_____

_____

_____

David was a king, but he was only a man. Yet, he provided for Mephibosheth abundantly as he honored and kept his covenant with Jonathan. Mephibosheth did not earn the favor of King David. Favor was granted him simply because of the covenant.

Our Deliverer is not merely a man like David. We serve Jesus, Our Covenant-Keeping King, and He is more than able and willing to meet all of our needs.

Yes, Jesus is Our King and He will never fail to keep His covenant with us. And His grace has provided a getaway out of Lo Debar.

The lasting and eternal covenant Jesus made with us was sealed by His precious blood when He willingly died on a cross for our sins. He provided forgiveness, restoration and renewed fellowship with God.

Jesus is our Mediator and High Priest. And He personally guarantees that this covenant is sure for all who receive Him as Savior.

> This makes Jesus the guarantee of a far better way between us and God—one that really works! A new covenant. Earlier there were a lot of priests, for they died and had to be replaced. But Jesus' priesthood is permanent. He's there from now to eternity to save everyone who comes to God through him, always on the job to speak up for them. So now we have a high priest who perfectly fits our needs: completely holy, uncompromised by sin, with authority extending as high as God's presence in heaven itself. Unlike the other high priests, he doesn't have to offer sacrifices for his own sins every day before he can get around to us and our sins. He's done it, once and for all: offered up *himself* as the sacrifice. The law appoints as high priests men who are never able to get the job done right. But this intervening command of God, which came later, appoints the Son, who is absolutely, eternally perfect (Hebrews 7:22-28 MSG).

We have an eternal, everlasting Covenant, not made by man. Our Covenant is from God, guaranteed by Jesus Christ, Our King.

Let's reflect a moment. In last week's lesson, one of the things we discussed was the importance of walking in the light of the redemptive revelation of Jesus Christ. We cannot afford to alter or dilute the truth of whom Jesus is. We cannot compromise when it comes to the Word of God. We must settle the questions that may arise in our minds that dispute the knowledge of God.

Read again these powerful verses we have already discussed in **Colossians 3:15** and **2 Corinthians 10:3-5**. These passages are crucial to a healthy thought life. They are so important and reading them often is imperative.

> And let the peace (soul harmony which comes) from Christ rule (act as umpire continually) in your hearts [deciding and

settling with finality all questions that arise in your minds, in that peaceful state] to which as [members of Christ's] one body you were also called [to live]. And be thankful (appreciative), [giving praise to God always] (Colossians 3:15 AMPC).

We are to settle with *finality* all questions that arise in our minds concerning our faith. We are to continually guard against imaginations, arguments and thoughts that attempt to alter our knowledge of God.

For though we walk in the flesh, we do not war after the flesh: (For the weapons of our warfare are not carnal, but mighty through God to the pulling down of strongholds;) Casting down imaginations, and every high thing that exalteth itself against the knowledge of God, and bringing into captivity every thought to the obedience of Christ (2 Corinthians 10:3-6 KJV). *What you allow, you Promote.*

I must always remember that *my mentality becomes my reality*.

Make it a habit to replace any negative thoughts with the true revelation of who He is. True revelation of Jesus Christ comes not from flesh and blood but from Our Father in Heaven.

Hold tightly to the revelation you have been given. You cannot waiver in your view of Jesus Christ. If you do, *Lo Debar will have a hold on you*. You will linger and ultimately reside there without accepting the full revelation of Christ. When you become unstable in your walk, it may indicate double-mindedness. And an unstable walk will take you to the wrong destination.

If any of you lacks wisdom, let him ask of God, who gives to all liberally and without reproach, and it will be given to him. But let him ask in faith, with no doubting, for he who doubts is like a wave of the sea driven and tossed by the wind. For let not that man suppose that he will receive anything from the Lord; he is a double-minded man, unstable in all his ways (James 1:5-7 NKJV).

The enemy's battlefield is always the mind. Have a determined mindset. Stand firm in your faith without wavering.

Let's turn to the gospel of Matthew and look at this familiar story. Take a moment and read a conversation Jesus had with some of His closest friends and disciples.

In **Matthew 16:13-19**, Jesus wanted to hear their response to perhaps the most important question ever asked: ***"But who do you say that I am?"***

> When Jesus came to the region of Caesarea Philippi, he asked his disciples, "Who do people say the Son of Man is?" They replied, "Some say John the Baptist; others say Elijah; and still others, Jeremiah or one of the prophets." "But what about you?" he asked. "Who do you say I am?" Simon Peter answered, "You are the Christ, the Son of the living God." Jesus replied, "Blessed are you, Simon son of Jonah, for this was not revealed to you by man, but by my Father in heaven. And I tell you that you are Peter, and on this rock I will build my church, and the gates of Hades will not overcome it. I will give you the keys of the kingdom of heaven; whatever you bind on earth will be bound in heaven, and whatever you loose on earth will be loosed in heaven (Matthew 16:13-19 NIV).

Jesus replied to Peter's response in **Matthew 16:17** with this statement. "Blessed are you, Simon son of Jonah, for this was not revealed to you by man, but by my Father in heaven."

Think about true revelation:

- *Revelation comes from God.*
- *Revelation requires a response.*
- *The greater the revelation, the less the reservation.*

The ***response*** and acceptance of that revelation causes us to become a Christian and a true believer of Jesus Christ. We are able to say with confidence, in absolute, unwavering faith just as Peter did, **"You are the Christ, the Son of the Living God!"**

Take a moment and praise God in a written prayer for the wonderful revelation you have been given concerning Christ!

The privilege of knowing Christ with greater revelation is promised for those who purposefully spend time in His presence and in the Word. He wants us to know the sweetness of His companionship. He desires for us to know the depth of His covenant.

> The secret [of the sweet, satisfying companionship] of the Lord have they who fear (revere and worship) Him, and He will show them His covenant and reveal to them its [deep, inner] meaning (Psalms 25:14 AMPC).

The greater the revelation, the less the reservation. The more you know about Him, the more you love Him. And the more you love Him, the more you want to share Him with others.

Yes, we all need to look again and evaluate the truth of this statement: *"You are the Christ, the Son of the Living God!"*

He is our Covenant-Keeping King.

If you can make that declaration in faith, Lo Debar has no lasting hold on you. You will have seasons and journeys walking through your Lo Debar, but you will not *reside* there.

95

Let's read this beloved Psalm and remember that we are going "through" not "residing in" the valley.

> The Lord is my shepherd; I shall not want. He makes me to lie down in green pastures; He leads me beside the still waters. He restores my soul; He leads me in the paths of righteousness For His name's sake. Yea, though I walk through the valley of the shadow of death, I will fear no evil; For You are with me; Your rod and Your staff, they comfort me. You prepare a table before me in the presence of my enemies; You anoint my head with oil; My cup runs over. Surely goodness and mercy shall follow me All the days of my life; And I will dwell in the house of the Lord Forever (Psalm 23:1-6 NKJV).

Notice in this beautiful Psalm of David, that The Lord, Our Shepherd and Covenant Keeping King. The Good Shepherd:

- *Provides for us*
- *Gives us a place of rest*
- *Restores our soul*
- *Leads us in the right paths*
- *Removes all fear*
- *Assures us of His presence*
- *Comforts us*
- *Prepares a table for us*
- *Anoints us*
- *Fills us to overflowing*
- *Declares goodness and mercy over us for everyday of our life*
- *And promises us a place with Him forever*

Take a moment and praise Jesus for His faithfulness to walk you through your seasons of darkness. He will never leave you in Lo Debar. If while you are there He actually will minister to you.

As Christians, committed and dedicated followers of Jesus Christ, we must always remember the importance of remaining faithful to Him while passing through our season of darkness.

Remember, it is the darkness in where the enemy comes and tries to raise questions, attempting to make us fear and doubt. But our resolute faithfulness stands as our declaration to Satan, and to everyone around us, that we believe our Covenant- Keeping King is able and willing to see us through. It will cause the light of truth in us to radiate. ***When our light shines, it will help light the pathway for someone abiding in Lo Debar; a permanent resident—not just passing through.*** The Light of Jesus Christ will give them a way out. We are called to be His hand extended, letting our light shine for the sake of the broken and hurting.

As Christians, we must always be mindful of the broken and wounded around us.

In **2 Samuel 9**, we read that a servant of the house of Saul named Ziba knew where to find Mephibosheth. Ziba was aware that the broken and outcast son of Jonathan was in Lo Debar. Interestingly, Ziba's name means *"army, fight, strength."* I believe there is an "army rising up" in the church; a dedicated and strong army committed to fight, bringing the broken out of Lo Debar to the House of the King.

With purpose, we must be aware of those in our sphere of influence. Reach out to those hurting and in need of the Light you have been given. Share the redemptive revelation of Jesus Christ without reservation to others. What a joy it is to know you helped lead someone out of darkness to the glorious Light of Jesus Christ.

Aren't you thankful someone told you about Him?

*Read **Luke 10:2**. Then, write a prayer asking for the Lord of the harvest to send forth workers into His harvest field. As you pray, ask The Lord to make you always willing to be one of those workers.*

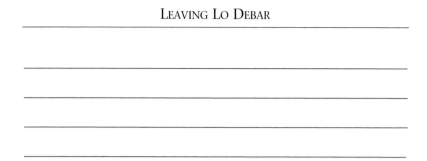

We are called to be that army, willing to fight for the Kingdom and to work to reach the lost. We must share our faith and the wonderful truth of salvation through Christ with those abiding in darkness.

We are not saved by our works, but our works may help someone else get saved!

Take a few moments to meditate on these verses.

> For the grace of God has appeared that offers salvation to all people. It teaches us to say, "No" to ungodliness and worldly passions, and to live self-controlled, upright and godly lives in this present age (Titus 2:11-12 NIV).

Grace is the gift of God, a gift that keeps on giving, teaching us to say "no" to the very things that will cause us to detour to and linger in Lo Debar. Remember that we lead and disciple others by our example.

This amazing, sufficient grace of God offers salvation freely, and it also instructs and teaches us daily. Most importantly, the application of those instructions enables us to live godly lives in this present age.

Yes! The grace of Jesus is our "getaway" from Lo Debar.

Let's present Jesus to them, Our Covenant-Keeping King. His great grace provides their way out of Lo Debar.

If you are introducing someone for the first time, what do you say about them? You usually put a lot of thought into it, commenting on some of their qualities and accomplishments.

When introducing others to Christ, what should we tell them about Our King? Who is this King of Glory, the One who can lead them out of the bondage of sin and the desolation of Lo Debar?

Who is this King of glory? The Lord strong and mighty, The Lord mighty in battle (Psalm 24:8, NKJV).

Yes, The Lord, Our King, is strong and mighty, and **He is so much more.**

It is impossible with the limitations of our vocabulary and finiteness to adequately answer the question, *"Who is this King of Glory?"* It is like trying to describe a beautiful color you have never seen. It is like attempting to sing a song you have never heard. He is beyond sight, sound and comprehension. The benefits and blessings of the Covenant He made with us are immeasurable.

The Word says this Gift of God is "indescribable."

Now thanks be to God for His Gift, [precious] beyond telling [His indescribable, inexpressible, free Gift] (2 Corinthians 9:15, AMPC)!

Praise God for His Gift, precious beyond our ability to tell—the indescribable, inexpressible, free Gift of His amazing, saving grace through Jesus Christ!

His Name alone brings comfort. Why? His Name—the Name of Jesus—encompasses all of who He is. It incorporates all the descriptions we have of Him and even those we are unable to grasp or express.

Saying the Name of Jesus ministers to the hurting. Speaking it in faith and under his authority can heal the sick. The Name of Jesus causes the demons of hell and darkness to tremble while, at the same time, giving peace and sweet assurance to His children.

Pause a moment and say His Name!

Speak it from your heart. Speaking His Name brings inexplicable comfort! His perfect peace that passes all understanding begins to flood your heart.

Yes, the Name of Jesus is beautiful to those who know Him as Savior and King. Calling on His Name is the pathway to salvation and the way out of Lo Debar.

For whoever calls on the name of the Lord shall be saved (Romans 10:13 NKJV).

His Name is a place of safety for the righteous.

> The name of the Lord is a strong tower; the [consistently] righteous man [upright and in right standing with God] runs into it and is safe, high [above evil] and strong (Proverbs 18:10 AMPC).

Calling on His Name assures us of the presence of Our Wonderful Counselor, Our Mighty God, Everlasting Father and Our Prince of Peace.

> For to us a Child is born, to us a Son is given; and the government shall be upon His shoulder, and His name shall be called Wonderful Counselor, Mighty God, Everlasting Father [of Eternity], Prince of Peace (Isaiah 9:6 AMPC).

Isaiah prophesied that through the power of His Name, everything we would need in this life and in the life to come would be supplied.

Do you need a Counselor? Do you need advice or direction? Do you need a Mighty God who can deliver you and put your life back in order? Do you need an Everlasting Father who is faithful and careful to watch over and protect and provide for you? Do you need the Prince of Peace to speak to your storm and calm your fears?

Say His Name! His Name, a "one word prayer" that, when prayed from the hearts of His children, summons all the help of Heaven. When prayed, it invokes the power and authority of Our Immeasurable, Unlimited, and Indescribable Covenant-Keeping King.

He is your "very present help in time of need."

Satan hates it when you call on His Name, because salvation comes through the name of Jesus; salvation from your sin, sorrow, sickness and situations. The kingdom of darkness will not overcome the power of His Name.

> And there is salvation in and through no one else, for there is no other name under heaven given among men by and in which we must be saved (Acts 4:12 AMPC).

There is no name given greater than or even comparable to the Name of Jesus!

> And being found in appearance as a man, he humbled himself and became obedient to death—even death on a cross! Therefore God exalted him to the highest place and gave him the name that is above every name, that at the name of Jesus every knee should bow, in heaven and on earth and under the earth, and every tongue confess that Jesus Christ is Lord, to the glory of God the Father (Philippians 2:8-11 NIV).

Speaking the Name of Jesus calls on all the authority and attributes of that glorious name. Let's look at just a *few* of the descriptions given in the Word of God concerning Jesus. He is:

- *The Alpha & Omega (Revelation 1:8; 22:13)*
- *Author and Perfector of Our Faith (Hebrews 12:2)*
- *The Bread of Life (John 6:35; 6:48)*
- *Our Coming Bridegroom (Matthew 9:15)*
- *The Chief Cornerstone (Ephesians 2:20)*
- *Our Deliverer (Romans 11:26)*
- *Immanuel (Isaiah 9:6; Matthew 1:23)*

- *Good Shepherd (John 10:11, 14)*
- *Holy One (Acts 3:14)*
- *High Priest (Hebrews 2:17)*
- *King of Kings and Lord of lords (1 Timothy 6:15)*
- *Lamb of God (John 1:29)*
- *Light of the World (John 8:12)*
- *Lord of All (Acts 10:36)*
- *Mediator (1 Timothy 2:5)*
- *Prince of Peace (Isaiah 9:6)*
- *The Rock (1 Corinthians 10:4)*
- *Resurrection and the Life (John 11:25)*
- *Our Savior (Matthew 1:21; Luke 2:11)*
- *The Way, Truth and the Life (John 14:6)*
- *He is the Word (John 1:1; 1 John 5:7-8)*

Take a moment to read this list again. Pause and praise Jesus, Your Covenant-Keeping King, for His faithfulness to you.

Thank Him that His sufficient grace strengthens you when you walk through the places of darkness. Then express heartfelt gratitude to Him for providing **the Great Grace Getaway from Lo Debar.**

Speak the Name of Jesus. That "one-word prayer" that says it all.

Let's look at one of the most powerful declaration Jesus made concerning Himself:

Jesus said to them, "Most assuredly, I say to you, before Abraham was, I AM (John 8:58, NKJV).

When Jesus made this statement, the Jews who heard Him wanted to stone Him for blasphemy. They knew He was referencing the revelation Moses had proclaimed concerning God, and, now, Jesus was identifying Himself with the unchanging God of the Old Testament.

Then Moses said to God, "Indeed, when I come to the children of Israel and say to them, 'The God of your fathers has sent me to you,' and they say to me, 'What is His name?' what shall I say to them?" And God said to Moses, "I AM WHO I AM." And He said, "Thus you shall say to the children of Israel, 'I AM has sent me to you (Exodus 3:13 NKJV).

In the Gospel of John, (the NKJV) alone, Jesus declared:

- *"I am the bread of life," John 6:35.*
- *"I am the Light of the world," John 8:12.*
- *"I am the door," John 10:9.*
- *"I am the good shepherd," John 10:11.*
- *"I am the resurrection and the life," John 11:25.*
- *"I am the way, the truth and the life," John 14:6.*
- *"I am the true vine," John 15:1.*

He is more than enough. Our Covenant-Keeping King is all we need.

No journey through Lo Debar; no season of darkness, sin, sorrow, sickness or situation is greater or stronger that Our Jesus.

Just as David did for Mephibosheth, Jesus will remember His covenant of grace and mercy! Let's look at how mercy is defined in the *Amplified Version* in **2 Samuel 9:3.**

> The king said, Is there not still someone of the house of Saul to whom I may show the [unfailing, unsought, unlimited] mercy and kindness of God? Ziba replied, Jonathan has yet a son who is lame in his feet (2 Samuel 9:3 AMPC).

The **Unfailing, Unsought and Unlimited** mercy of God is ours through Jesus Christ. His mercy is:

- *Unfailing—always victorious over sin and judgement.*

103

- *Unsought—we feel "undeserving" so we do not seek or expect it.*
- *Unlimited—it is without measure and never runs out.*

POINTS TO PONDER

Because of a covenant made with Jonathan; David extended grace. And his mercy provided for Mephibosheth a seat at the table of the king. **Hebrews 7:22** reminds us of a better covenant than any man could ever provide.

Jesus will always honor His covenant. He reached out with grace and mercy to bring us out of darkness.

The covenant Jesus made was sealed and secured with His shed blood on Calvary. When Jesus cried out on the cross "It is finished!" **(John 19:30)** I do not believe He was not announcing His death. Rather, He was declaring the completion of the covenant. The sacrificial Lamb of God had fulfilled the requirements to purchase our redemption once and for all.

The Word in **Mark 15:33** tells us that darkness covered the whole land while Jesus was suffering and dying, but deliverance was coming. The darkness, caused by sin and separation, would be forever destroyed for all who stepped into the new covenant of Christ.

The message of **Mark 15:38** reminds us that at the moment Jesus declared "It is finished," the veil in the Temple was torn in two from top to bottom. This veil had separated the Holy of Holies from common man. The Holy of Holies contained the Ark of the Covenant, the symbol of God's relationship with man.

This veil was huge and heavy made of fine linen of blue, purple and scarlet yarn. It was embroidered with gold cherubim. But when Jesus cried out, the veil was torn in two, giving all of us access to God. We were invited into His presence through the death of Jesus. His covenant—His grace—became the gateway to God.

On top of the Ark was the Mercy Seat where the blood of sacrificial animals was sprinkled for the sins of the people. The torn veil allowed entrance to the place known as the Mercy Seat. The Covenant-Keeping King invited us to the Mercy Seat, the place where God promised to meet us.

Mephibosheth was invited to the "mercy seat" provided at the table of King David. At this table, Mephibosheth's brokenness was covered by the grace of the king. Yes, grace covered Mephibosheth's weakness. Neither David nor anyone else seated at the table drew attention to his brokenness. Rather, David, through the eyes of grace, saw Mephibosheth as one of his own sons.

Like Mephibosheth at King David's table, we have been given a seat at the table of Our King because of the mercy of Jesus Christ. We have permanent access to the Mercy Seat which was once hidden behind the veil. Because of His grace, our sins, faults and failures are covered. Jesus looks at us through eyes of mercy. And we are His sons and daughters.

Our Covenant-Keeping King provided the Great Grace Getaway from Lo Debar.

When darkness seems to override your joy and peace, remember the way out is secure. You are just passing through.

As we conclude this week's lesson, let's pause and say the name of Our Covenant-Keeping King!

Say the name of Jesus! Yes, it is that "one word prayer" when prayed from the heart of His children summons all the help of Heaven. It is the prayer that calls on our Immeasurable, Unlimited and Indescribable Covenant-Keeping King.

- He is your ever present help in time of need.
- His grace is sufficient.
- His presence is promised.
- His covenant is sealed.

As you study and journal this week, spend time reflecting on **Psalm 23.** *Think of the blessings of walking with your Covenant Keeping King. Rejoice in the assurance that He is more than enough for any journey you may take through Lo Debar. His grace has provided a way out.* ***Say the Name!***

Week 6

POWER TRUTH

I Am Who The I Am Says I Am!

Leaving Lo Debar

The enemy wants to rob you of your spiritual identity given through Christ. We must guard against **spiritual identity theft** and remember who we are to God.

Meditate and memorize this powerful verse.

But as many as received Him, to them He gave the right to become children of God, to those who believe in His name (John 1:12, NKJV).

Rejoice because you have been given the right to become and be called a child of God. Praise God because even though you may pass through Lo Debar; you will never reside there.

I Am Who The I Am Says I Am!

Leaving Lo Debar
John 1:12

But as many as received Him, to them He gave the right to become children of God, to those who believe in His name (John 1:12, NKJV).

IN LAST WEEK'S LESSON, we discussed Our Covenant-Keeping King. We looked at passages of Scripture which helped us understand the authority and attributes of Jesus.

We discussed the power and comfort coming to us by simply speaking His Name. ***Yes, His Name is a "one word prayer" when prayed from the heart of His children summons all the help of Heaven.***

"Jesus"—the prayer that calls on Our Immeasurable, Unlimited, and Indescribable Covenant-Keeping King.

And He is faithful to hear us when we call on Him. Calling on His Name brings His presence, His peace and His power.

We take comfort in knowing that the **Unfailing, Unsought and Unlimited** mercy of God is ours through Jesus Christ.

Throughout this study, we have looked at various passages of Scripture that deal with how we are to view ourselves. We have been exploring the different ways we may end up in Lo Debar. As we have already discussed, one of the pathways to Lo Debar is low self-worth.

This week we will look further into God's great love for us and how He **identifies** us accordingly.

Our theme verse for this week, **John 1:12**, reminds us that because we have received Christ, we are given the right to become His children. It is so important to grasp and hold tightly to this powerful promise.

Just as we have discussed the importance of guarding and keeping the revelation of Christ in the forefront of our mind; we must also see ourselves as He sees us in order to fully walk in freedom.

POINTS TO PONDER

Several months ago, our pastor was preaching a powerful message and he made a statement that went straight to my heart. If you have ever had the privilege of hearing Bishop Kenneth Murphy preach, you know he keeps your attention. So that particular Sunday was no exception. He was preaching on the unwavering faithfulness of God to His children. He reminded us that in trying times, we do not need to "hear" the accusing and condemning voice of the enemy. Instead, we need to always remember what God says about us. And then he made this statement.

"I am who the I AM says I am!"

I will never forget that declaration It made me more determined to look to the Word of God and take time to seek out "who the I AM says I am!"

The list I am providing from that search through the Word is **far** from complete. There is so much that could be added, but I have chosen some of my favorite passages that ministered to me. I want to share them with you and I pray you are blessed.

As you read the list, remember, when you do experience seasons of discouragement; you are passing through Lo Debar. ***Determine never to be a resident there.*** Be encouraged that your season of sorrow will end; because you are a child of the Covenant-Keeping King, and you ARE who He says you are.

WHO AM I?
- **I am a child of God (John 1:12).**
- **I am blameless and free of accusations (Colossians 1:22).**
- **I am born of God and Satan cannot touch me (1 John 4:8).**
- **I am a partaker of His divine nature (2 Peter 1:3-4).**
- **I am free from condemnation (Romans 8:1).**
- **I am a joint heir with Christ (Romans 8:17).**
- **I am called by name and I am His own (Isaiah 43:1).**
- **I am loved with an everlasting love (Jeremiah 31:3).**
- **I am the apple of His eye (Zechariah 2:8).**
- **I am His friend (John 15:15).**
- **I am Blessed (Ephesians 1:3).**
- **I am wonderfully made (Psalm 139:14).**
- **I am justified and redeemed (Romans 3:24).**
- **I am a citizen of Heaven (Philippians 3:20).**
- **I am Holy and Blameless (Ephesians 1:4).**
- **I am Forgiven and Sanctified (Ephesians 1:7).**
- **I am His ambassador (2 Corinthians 5:20).**

- **I am the recipient of eternal life (John 3:16).**
- **I am blessed with abundant life (John 10:10).**
- **I am an overcomer by the Blood of Jesus (Revelation 12:11).**
- **I am a friend of Jesus Christ (John 15:15).**
- **I am an enemy of Satan (1 Peter 5:8).**
- **I am victorious through Him (1 Corinthians 15:57).**
- **I am more than a conqueror (Romans 8:37).**

Each one of these statements stands alone and is sufficient to defeat the enemy. *Pick one.* Read it aloud. You may sense the presence of God comfort and encourage as you embrace what He had declared about you.

What attribute on the list of "Who Am I" spoke to your heart the most? Write it down and read the verse related to it. Why do you think it ministered to you?

_____

_____

_____

_____

_____

_____

My prayer is that you will learn from the Word of God exactly how the Lord sees and identifies you. I pray that you are strengthened and encouraged daily as you meditate on these declarations and the blessings that come with them.

Yes, it is so important to see how God identifies us and how we hold on to our God-given identity.

We have all heard the phrase **"identity theft"** and we understand how important it is to guard our identity from would-be thieves.

It is critical to protect yourself from identity theft. Once stolen, the access to your financial and personal information is in the hands of cyber thieves. Your identity becomes theirs to make exorbitant purchases, to obtain other credit cards and to invade all your hard-earned accounts. Then your good name may be tainted and most difficult to recover. Of course, once your finances are depleted, your credit rating destroyed, and your identity totally discredited, you are left with a mess to clean up. In the process the identity thief leaves you in brokenness and ruin, and without conscience, he/she never looks back.

So, absolutely, we must utilize extra measures to protect and secure our identity from theft.

But let's think about our **spiritual identity.** The devil, the enemy of our soul, would much rather rob you of your spiritual identity than just mere possessions you might have acquired in this life. So, it is more important to take extra precautions to protect the spiritual identity we have obtained through Christ.

We must be on guard against the enemy. Remember, **John 10:10** clearly declares the thief's agenda.

> The thief does not come except to steal, and to kill, and to destroy. I have come that they may have life, and that they may have it more abundantly John 10:10 NKJV).

Since the enemy comes to steal, kill and destroy, we must guard against spiritual identity theft.

Satan wants to steal your true identity, because in doing so, he intends to kill your dreams and destroy your goals. Just like the modern day identity thief treats your credit and finances, the devil wants to deplete you of your worth and leave you in brokenness and ruin spiritually. He certainly does not want you to walk in the authority given to a son or daughter of God. ***He desires to make you a permanent resident in Lo Debar.***

Another story in the Old Testament gives us a great example of an attempt to steal the spiritual identity of God's people.

Let's take a few moments to read the passage recorded in **Daniel 1:1-7**, focusing on verses 6 and 7.

> In the third year of the reign of Jehoiakim king of Judah, Nebuchadnezzar king of Babylon came to Jerusalem and besieged it. And the Lord gave Jehoiakim king of Judah into his hand, with some of the articles of the house of God, which he carried into the land of Shinar to the house of his god; and he brought the articles into the treasure house of his god. Then the king instructed Ashpenaz, the master of his eunuchs, to bring some of the children of Israel and some of the king's descendants and some of the nobles, young men in whom there was no blemish, but good-looking, gifted in all wisdom, possessing knowledge and quick to understand, who had ability to serve in the king's palace, and whom they might teach the language and literature of the Chaldeans. And the king appointed for them a daily provision of the king's delicacies and of the wine which he drank, and three years of training for them, so that at the end of that time they might serve before the king. Now from among those of the sons of Judah were Daniel, Hananiah, Mishael, and Azariah. To them the chief of the eunuchs gave names: he gave Daniel the name Belteshazzar; to Hananiah, Shadrach; to Mishael, Meshach; and to Azariah, Abed-Nego (Daniel 1:1-7 NKJV).

In this account, we read how King Nebuchadnezzar of Babylon came to Jerusalem and stole from the temple great treasures and also took captive some of the "children of Israel and some of the king's descendants." Instructions were given by King Nebuchadnezzar to seek out the "gifted in all wisdom," his intent being to use them for his purposes and to make servants out of them in his palace.

114

Just as the enemy stole Mephibosheth's identity, he set out to do the same with these captives. Satan's goal is to do the same to you.

Let's notice something *very, very important* in this passage. In verse 6 we see the actual list of names of the four men taken into captivity: ***Daniel, Hananiah, Mishael and Azariah.***

It is so interesting that the enemy changed their names, respectively, to: ***Belteshazzar, Shadrach, Meshach and Abed-Nego.***

Why was it crucial to the enemy concerning these men to make it a priority to immediately change their names? Because their names represented who they really were in significance to their **spiritual identity.**

The name, Daniel, means ***"God is my judge."*** *(So, Daniel had no need to fear man!)*

The name, Hananiah, means ***"Jehovah is gracious."*** *(Hananiah trusted God's sufficient grace and favor were with him.)*

The name, Mishael, means ***"one who is like God."*** *(Mishael's nature and character were godly and righteous.)*

The name, Azariah, means ***"The Lord has helped."*** *(Azariah knew God had helped in the past and he was confident God would help in the present and future.)*

The Word in **Daniel 1:6** also tells us that these young men were ***"sons of Judah."*** And ***Judah means "praise."***

Let's put this into perspective. Standing before the enemy-- their captor--were four young men whose very names threatened the opposing king.

Their names also reveal so much. When we are saved we identify with each of the meanings of these names. Think of this. When we are redeemed we can declare that:

• Like Daniel, God is my judge and not the fear of man.

• Like Hananiah, I am saved because of God's gracious intervention on my behalf.

• Like Mishael, old things have passed away and my new nature is in Christ.

• Like Azariah, the Lord has helped me and will continually be at my side to assist again when I am in need.

So, I am planted in and am a member of the household of PRAISE.

NO WONDER THE KING CHANGED THEIR NAMES!

He attempted to steal their identity by labeling them with names representing pagan kings and rituals of the culture they were forced to live in.

But even though they were renamed by the enemy and referred to as Shadrach, Meshach and Abed-Nego, they did **not** forget who they really were! They maintained their spiritual identity. They held tightly to their roots in Judah.

Let's read a portion of the familiar account that we often refer to as *"The Story of the Three Hebrew Boys"* recorded in Daniel 3. In verses 1-12, we read how the king made a golden image, an idol, many believe it was in his likeness. Instructions were given that when certain music was played everyone was to bow and worship the image. If anyone refused, they would be thrown into a fiery furnace.

Read in verses 13-15 King Nebuchadnezzar's angry reaction when word came to him that the Hebrew boys refused to bow. Please note what is worth mentioning here is some theologians believe Daniel would have been "standing" right there with the three others, but he was on a separate mission for the king and not present at the time. Of course, we know Daniel stood strong in his faith and in his spiritual identity faithfully; especially in chapter 6 when facing his own lion's den.

Then Nebuchadnezzar, in rage and fury, gave the command to bring Shadrach, Meshach, and Abed-Nego. So they brought these men before the king. Nebuchadnezzar spoke, saying to them, "Is it true, Shadrach, Meshach, and Abed-Nego, that you do not serve my gods or worship the gold image which I have set up? Now if you are ready at the time you hear the sound of the horn, flute, harp, lyre, and psaltery, in symphony with all kinds of music, and you fall down and worship the image which I have made, good! But if you do not worship, you shall be cast immediately into the midst of a burning fiery furnace. And who is the god who will deliver you from my hands? (Daniel 3:13-15 NKJV).

Well! I think that was the "wrong question" to ask. I believe the Spirit of God was stirring on the inside of these young men, and they had already begun to ponder the answer to that very question.

Who is this God who will deliver us? Oh, let us just think about Him!

He is:
• Omniscient (all knowing)
• Omnipotent (all powerful)
• Omnipresent (always present)

He is:
• Jehovah – Jireh, Our Provider
• Jehovah – Rapha, Our Healer
• Jehovah – Nissi, Our Banner
• Jehovah – Shalom, Our Peace

When the enemy comes to you and attempts to make you doubt in the face of your greatest fear; remember who your God is.

My God is:
• *My Healer (Isaiah 53:5)*
• *My Shield (Psalm 3:3)*

- *My Rock of Ages (Ps. 28:1)*
- *My Savior (Acts 13:23)*
- *He is my very present help in my times of trouble (Psalm 46:1).*
- *He is the Great I Am (John 8:58).*
- *The Alpha and Omega - The First and The Last (Rev 22:13)*
- *He is The Living Bread (John 6:32).*
- *The True Vine (John 15:5)*
- *He is my Wonderful Counselor, Everlasting Father (Isaiah 9:6).*
- *Prince of Peace (Isaiah 9:6).*
- *He is my Refuge and Fortress (Psalm 91:2).*
- *He is my Light in Darkness (John 1:5).*
- *He is my Advocate (1 John 2:1).*
- *He is my Lord of lords and King of kings (1Timothy 6:15).*
- *He is coming back for me (John 14:3).*

Which item about the attributes of Our God brought you the most comfort? Read the verse connected to it and write what it means to you.

_____

_____

_____

_____

_____

_____

_____

Now, take a moment for a Praise Break. I know you want to. He is worthy. ***What an awesome God we serve!***

It was the revelation of their God and the determination of the Hebrew boys to hold on to their ***spiritual identity*** through

Him, enabling them to stand; even while in the enemy's camp, facing their greatest fear.

> Shadrach, Meshach, and Abed-Nego answered and said to the king, "O Nebuchadnezzar, we have no need to answer you in this matter. If that is the case, our God whom we serve is able to deliver us from the burning fiery furnace, and He will deliver us from your hand, O king. But if not, let it be known to you, O king, that we do not serve your gods, nor will we worship the gold image which you have set up (Daniel 3:16-18 NKJV).

They were confident in their identity. They had not allowed an attempt of *spiritual identity theft* to rob themselves of whom they were in God. Their confidence **in God** and **in their identity** is apparent in the above verses as they declared:

- ***Our God whom we serve is able to deliver us.***
- ***He will deliver us from your hand.***
- ***We do NOT serve your gods.***
- ***We will NOT worship the gold image you set up.***

They knew who they were and their identity was rooted in their love and faithfulness to God; and it made no provision for compromise.

We read in verses 19-23 how the king was so angry with their response and refusal to bow to the idol, and he did just as he said he would. The king ordered them bound and thrown into the flaming furnace. But we rejoice when we read the outcome. Read verses 24-27.

> Suddenly the king jumped up and shouted, "Weren't only three men tied up and thrown into the fire?" "Yes, Your Majesty," the people answered. "But I see four men walking around in the fire," the king replied. "None of them is tied up or harmed, and the fourth one looks like a god." Nebuchadnezzar went closer to the flaming furnace and said to the three young men, "You servants of the Most High God, come out at once!"

They came out, and the king's high officials, governors, and advisors all crowded around them. The men were not burned, their hair wasn't scorched, and their clothes didn't even smell like smoke (Daniel 3:24-27 CEV).

The king saw The Son of God with them. The enemy sees Him present with you. The only thing destroyed in the fire was the binding that had been put on them. ***They were free, even IN the fire.*** They were not hurt. Not a hair on their heads was scorched, and they didn't even smell like smoke.

And when they passed through the fire and their trial, they came through assured of whom their God was and who they were to Him.

They were secure in their God and in their identity.

Say it with me..."I am who the I AM says I am!"

Remember, while passing through your Lo Debar, your valley, your season of darkness, your own fiery trial; that you have been identified with Christ. You have been given the right to become and be called a child of God. Your identity is in Him.

Do not receive in your heart any negative words that are spoken over you, especially during your journey through Lo Debar. Do not let people, or the enemy, rob you of your identity. Do not allow their opinions to alter how you see yourself or how you see or perceive God.

Some people truly mean well. Not all "negative words" are intended to be hurtful. There were probably some people who would have encouraged the Hebrew boys by suggesting *"Just bow. God will understand. He knows your heart."* They meant well.

However, if an opinion given to you is not Spirit-led and, if it encourages you to **compromise**; dismiss it as nothing more than what it is—an opinion.

Comments or thoughts from well-meaning people, if you heed them without seeking God first, can actually delay your

God-given purpose and alter your intended course. We all are vulnerable and have to guard against our desire to take, when offered, what appears to be the "quickest way out" of Lo Debar.

Perhaps you are in a season that is trying and pressing, as you stand before your "fiery furnace," but you know in your heart it will end well if you are faithful. The Holy Spirit is encouraging you to "hold on" and endure a little longer. Things are about to change. You can feel it in your heart.

Maybe a friend offers a suggestion to "try a new thing." Perhaps they advise you to take a new position or a different job.

Maybe you are in ministry and they see the stress you are under and suggest you "let go of this ministry and step into the next." Maybe they say things like, "you have paid your dues, move on to better things."

Perhaps someone is giving you "advice on your marriage" or even on your financial affairs. If it does not agree with what the Word directs, do not receive their instructions, opinions or advice.

Do not forget who you are. You are an overcomer through Christ. If it is not God-ordained or in His timing, do not lose your identity by taking the easy way out.

Timing is crucial in making decisions. If the timing is wrong, you will actually lose ground and prolong your stay in Lo Debar.

JUST A THOUGHT FROM MY HEART

Free kittens are always easy to find. Free opinions are just like those free kittens—sweet and appealing. But, if the opinion does not line up with The Word of God, do not take it home and nurture it. Leave the opinion. Take the kitten. You will be much better off with the cat. It is easier to change a litter box than to clean up a mess made from a misguided point of view, regardless of the good intentions of the one giving it.

In the account of the Hebrew boys, we rejoice when we read that the fire did not harm them, and they did not even smell like smoke. The only thing destroyed was what bound them. They were free **IN the fire** because they knew who they were, and they knew who was walking with them.

They never forgot the answer to the question the king asked: ***"And who is this god who will deliver you from my hands?"*** They never forgot their true identities. They refused to take to heart the labels the king had given them.

In your season through Lo Debar, the enemy may try to label you "discouraged." He may call you "defeated" or "fearful," but do not receive his labels or names. ***Remember who you are.***

In this last lesson of our study, let's reflect back over what we have discussed.

We know the importance of not walking in condemnation. We are determined to be free from the accusations of the enemy. There is NOW no condemnation in us. We will not enter Lo Debar through *the Condemnation Connection.*

We have determined not to walk in un-forgiveness, birthed by blaming others for our situations. We lay down blame and extend grace and mercy to those who have hurt us. We will not walk through *the Blame Game Gateway* again.

We will be confident during our season of darkness, caused by any circumstances beyond our control. Our God will bring us through. We will rest in complete assurance and peace; expecting our Deliverer from the Darkness of Lo Debar to be present every moment. He will lovingly minister to us while we are there.

And we refuse to compromise and dim the light of truth. We will not reside in darkness caused by compromise! We will not adjust or adapt to the darkness. We will not settle for less that His glorious truth. The Light of His Word will guide us. My mentality becomes my reality, so I will guard my mind against compromising the revelation of Who He is.

We will always remember that we walk with our **Covenant-Keeping King** and He is the way out of Lo Debar. When I walk with **The Way**, I can never get lose my way or end up in the wrong place.

And I will declare that **I am who the I AM says I am.** I will guard my spiritual identity and the enemy will not steal it from me

Say it again with me one more time, "I am who the I AM says I am!"

Take a moment and **Pray.**

PRAYER

"Heavenly Father, My Omniscient, Omnipotent, Omnipresent God, thank You that You loved me so much that You sent Your Only Son to die for my sins and redeem me. Thank You that You have made a way out of Lo Debar for me! Thank You that when I do pass through difficult places, You are faithful to walk with me every step of the way. You will never leave me or forsake me. You will lead me to your plan and purpose for me. Thank You that I can rest in the assurance that I am who You say I am! I am forever grateful to be given the right to be called your child. What a wonderful privilege and blessing. I love You, Lord. I know You will walk with me through my temporary seasons in Lo Debar, and I am so grateful that because of You, I do not have to reside there. Your grace and mercy have provided a way out."

In Jesus' name. Amen.

Now, praise Him from your heart for His tender love and care for you.

As you study and journal this week, remember to declare, I may have seasons and times in Lo Debar, but I will never take up residency

there. I am only passing through. ***Never staying—always leaving Lo Debar.***

Conclusion

I WILL ALWAYS remember hearing the story of an elderly woman who was on her death bed in the final days of her life. The doctor called the family in and told them it would not be long before her passing away. He said to her son who was beside her bed, "Say your goodbyes; she's sinking fast." She had been in a deep sleep and had spoken nothing for several days. But when she heard that statement, she managed to open her eyes and say, "Oh no, Doc, you're wrong! You can't sink when you're standing on Solid Rock." Those were her final words in this life.

Remember, when you experience your season through Lo Debar, you are firmly planted on Christ. Your foundation is sure.

The devil will say to you, *"This time through, you're going down; you're losing this battle; you're sinking!"*

Just as the elderly woman said, **You cannot sink when you are standing on Solid Rock.** I may slip and stumble and even fall… but I will NOT get off the Rock.

Read again this beloved passage:

> But as for me, I will look to the Lord and confident in Him I will keep watch; I will wait with hope and expectancy for the God of my salvation; my God will hear me. Rejoice not against me, O my enemy! When I fall, I shall arise; when I sit in darkness, the Lord shall be a light to me (Micah 7:7-8 AMPC).

But as for me, I will **look** to the Lord. I will be **confident** in Him. I will **watch** for Him. I will **wait** with hope and expectation. My God will hear me.

- **I will look.**
- **I will be confident.**

- **I will watch.**
- **I will wait.**

Remember this beautiful promise recorded in Isaiah 43:2.

> When you cross through deep rivers, I will be with you, and you won't drown. When you walk through the fire, you won't be burned or scorched by the flames (Isaiah 43.2 CEV).

This too shall pass. Yes, I may pass through Lo Debar, but I am already on my way out when I get there.

I will never settle in Lo Debar!